LIVING THE GOOD LIFE

MARK LOWERY, PH. D.

Living the *Good* Life

What Every Catholic
Needs to Know About
MORAL ISSUES

CHARIS

SERVANT PUBLICATIONS
ANN ARBOR, MICHIGAN

Charis books is an imprint of Servant Publications especially designed to serve
Roman Catholics.

> **Servant Publications—Mission Statement**
> We are dedicated to publishing books that spread the gospel of Jesus
> Christ, help Christians to live in accordance with that gospel, promote
> renewal in the church, and bear witness to Christian unity.

Unless otherwise noted, Scripture verses are from the Revised Standard
Version of the Bible, copyrighted 1946, 1952, 1971 by the Division of Christian
Education of the National Council of Churches of Christ in the USA. Used by
permission. Excerpts from the English translation of the Catechism of the
Catholic Church for use in the United States of America Copyright 1994,
United States Catholic Conference, Inc.-Libreria Editrice Vaticana. Used with
Permission.

Published by Servant Publications
P.O. Box 8617
Ann Arbor, Michigan 48107
www.servantpub.com

Cover design: Noah Pudgil Design Professionals

03 04 05 06 10 9 8 7 6 5 4 3 2 1

Printed in the United States of America
ISBN 1-56955-356-4

Library of Congress Cataloging-in-Publication Data

Lowery, Mark D.
  Living the good life : what every Catholic needs to know about moral
issues / Mark Lowery.
      p. cm.
Includes bibliographical references.
  ISBN 1-56955-356-4 (alk. paper)
  1. Christian ethics–Catholic authors. 2. Christian
ethics–Miscellanea. I. Title.
  BJ1249.L66 2003
  241'.042–dc21

                                                                    2003008274

CONTENTS

Introduction: Not Just Academic Reading / 7

1. Authentic Freedom and Conscience / 13

2. Truth Is Friendly to Us: The Meaning of Participated Theonomy / 37

3. "How Can It Be Wrong When It Feels So Good?": The Natural Law /53

4. The Natural Language of the Body / 75

5. Partaking in the Divine / 97

6. Disordered Goods: The Mystery of Sin / 123

7. The Nature of the Moral Act: Making Christ Present in History / 149

8. The Tough Cases / 177

9. "There Is No Upper Limit": The Virtues / 205

Conclusion: "Where Do I Go From Here?": To the Eucharist / 221
Notes / 225

Have you ever heard someone complain about academic, "bookish" theology, claiming that religion should primarily be about *living* a moral life instead of *analyzing* it? Scholars even have a "bookish" way of making that very claim: They say that *orthopraxis* (right practice) has priority over *orthodoxy* (right doctrine or right teaching).

In fact, both orthopraxis *and* orthodoxy are equally necessary. Unless doctrine is really lived out, it's useless in the final end—and I mean "final end" literally, as in, getting to heaven. But if *what* a person is living out is riddled with error, then all good intentions aside, that person will end up with a shabby moral life. So right doctrine (ortho*doxy*) needs to be completed in right practice (ortho*praxis*), and practice in turn needs to be informed by right doctrine.

The 1993 encyclical of Pope John Paul II entitled *Veritatis Splendor*—"The Splendor of the Truth"—certainly gives the reader the impression that its author held to this principle. It's all about living virtuously—in fact, the biblical parable of the rich young man is recalled at the outset as the perfect example of the person who hesitates before the full *living out* of the gospel. Yet in pondering the encyclical the reader is also struck by the importance of getting moral doctrine "just right." Why? Because a failure there can enslave a person to bad moral habits that make life a rough path with an uncertain destination.

The goal of my book is to serve as an introduction to the Church's moral vision. Not surprisingly, then, it frequently offers the reader opportunities to meditate on and to understand the text of *Veritatis Splendor*. As you read my book, I hope you'll consider reading that entire encyclical alongside it.

You'll also find here plenty of cross-references to the *Catechism of the Catholic Church* (hereafter cited as "CCC")[1], and to the work of St. Thomas Aquinas. Use the footnotes to discover which sections of St. Thomas' *Summa Theologica*[2] (easily accessible on the Internet) to pursue. In addition, after my response to some questions I provide information about where to look for relevant passages in these and other texts.

Those who wish to make use of additional resources can find a glossary, review questions, teaching aids, and additional materials for each chapter at the author's web site.[3]

Often when we think of moral theology, a range of concrete and disputatious issues comes to mind: the death penalty, new birth technologies, euthanasia and abortion, stem-cell research, contraception, homosexual acts, and the like. Yet all these contemporary debates on specific issues are usually manifestations of disagreements (however tacit) on the level of fundamental moral principles. For example, the person confused about contraception may well be more fundamentally confused about the nature of conscience and freedom; the person wondering about abortion and euthanasia may need to learn about the natural law; and the person perplexed by the complexities of sexuality may need to ponder the theology of the body and the relationship between body and soul.

For this reason, the best way to study specific issues is to begin on the level of fundamental principles. That's the approach of *Veritatis Splendor*, and it's the approach of this book as well. As illustrations, we've tucked in plenty of specific examples from bioethics, sexual ethics, and social ethics.

I hope reading this book helps clarify some things for you. Even more importantly, I hope, in the spirit of *Veritatis Splendor*, that it is of some small assistance in living what moral philosophers have long called "the good life." By that phrase, we don't mean a life filled with creature comforts, but rather a life that is morally good—a *virtuous* life.

Speaking of assistance, lots of people lent a hand with this book. Thanks in particular to Dr. Janet Smith and to a number of others who gave valuable suggestions: Jennifer Carrier, Sheryl Colmer, Suzanne Jacob, Amy Love, Les Maiman, Mary Lou Molitor, Argiro Morgan, and Bret Schanzenbach. Thanks to Ben Lowery for the diagams. Finally, I should identify the source of the important questions that provide the structure of the book as a conversation with an anonymous inquirer: These great challenges came originally from the numerous fine students I have worked with over the years at the University of Dallas. Thanks to all of you!

Pope John Paul II[4]

CA   *Centesimus Annus* (On the Hundreth Anniversary)

EV   *Evangelium Vitae* (The Gospel of Life)

FC   *Familiaris Consortio* (The Family in the Modern World)

LF   Letter to Families

SRS *Sollicitudo Rei Socialis* (On Social Concern)

VS   *Veritatis Splendor* (The Splendor of the Truth)[5]

Second Vatican Council (Vatican II)[6]

DH   *Dignitatis Humanae* (On Religious Freedom)

DV   *Dei Verbum* (On Divine Revelation)

GS   *Gaudium et Spes* (On the Church in the Modern World)

LG   *Lumen Gentium* (On the Church)

Q. Something's puzzling me. The Church teaches us that we have freedom and that we must follow our consciences. Then, the Church gives us moral norms that we should follow. What's the point, then, of freedom and conscience?

The trick is to understand properly the terms *freedom* and *conscience*—and they are perhaps *the* most misunderstood ideas today. "I am free to follow my conscience" often means "I can do what I want as long as I don't hurt anyone else." Perhaps you've been hurt by someone who thinks that way—or you certainly know someone who has. Time to dissect these terms!

If you ask a group of people to answer the question "Am I free?" you'll get some interesting answers, most of them only half true.

Some will say they are free because they have *free will* (also called "natural" or "psychological" freedom). They correctly emphasize that people are not solely conditioned by external forces (the environment) and internal forces (brain chemistry). We are not merely super-charged biochemical mechanisms, highly evolved animals. We can engage in *voluntary* acts.

Others will say they are free because they have *political* freedom, those freedoms allowed by their political regime such as freedom of religion, freedom of the press, and the like. And they might appreciate such political freedom so much that they would affirm the old slogan "Live free or die!" (New Hampshire's state motto).

Some people insist: "I'll use these freedoms just the way I want. I'll do it my way." We could say that such people are *autonomous*—they are "a law unto themselves." They believe that freedom means doing as we choose with our natural and political freedom (under the condition that "we don't hurt anybody else"—we'll analyze that one shortly). We can label this view, which absolutizes free will and political freedom, "secular freedom."

There's only one problem. Such "freedom" is really only a capacity or potentiality unless it is properly *used*. And people who use their freedom autonomously sooner or later find out they're not as free as they think. They quickly get enslaved to bad habits. If they're honest, they'll say things like "That was a bad choice; don't do what I did." They admit that they didn't use their freedom correctly—which means that, somewhere, there's a *right* way to use it.

True freedom, or authentic freedom, is the proper *use* of our free will and political freedom.[1] It is the freedom that comes from having aligned ourselves with the true and the good. Freedom means, ironically, being "bound" to the truth.

In one way this binding limits us—we no longer choose evil. But what a great kind of limitation! What person, having been enslaved to a bad habit, doesn't rejoice when that vice is conquered and is now "off limits"? This is true liberation!

We often hear the quote from St. Augustine: "Love God and do what you please." But we must keep in mind that he didn't mean "Do whatever you want." He meant that what pleases the authentically free person is in alignment with what God wills.

Authentic freedom—alignment with the will of God—opens a person to a more profound happiness than he or she would ever have imagined. No doubt the numerous options that come from secular freedom are no longer available to the authentically free person. But those options, while carrying a surface kind of excitement, never yield this profound happiness and inner freedom.

In becoming authentically free, we give up "optionality" but are rewarded abundantly with the genuine happiness that proceeds from a virtuous life.[2] For the Christian, this happiness is immeasurably increased by grace—an ever-deepening participation in the divine Trinitarian life. And such a gift of grace creates moral *beauty* in a person.[3]

True freedom, then, is a freedom *for* the good. It is in this true freedom that we find our dignity. We do not lose our uniqueness in aligning ourselves with the truth. We allow the fullness of our unique selves to flourish, resulting in true *individuality*.

Individual*ity* must be distinguished from individual*ism*, which results from the autonomous, or secular, view of freedom. Individuality allows the true self to flourish in harmony with transcendent truth; individualism makes the self the arbiter of the truth (just what Adam and Eve did in the garden—see *VS* 35).

I hope you like analogies, because this book is filled with them. Here's one to consider: Imagine you're fascinated by a sport, such as golf, or a musical instrument such as the saxophone. Experts make these skills look easy, and your first instinct is to think: *I bet I can do that, give me a try at it.*

Nevertheless, you quickly discover that, although you're free to give it a try, such freedom must be properly—and arduously—ordered. Otherwise, you live with the frustration of horrid shots or dissonant notes. Once you wisely recognize the need to discover the objective and transcendent truth about the nature of a golf swing or the way music is played, true happiness and enjoyment ensues.

Interestingly, it's only after aligning yourself with that truth that you can even begin to think about uniqueness and individuality. Every professional golfer will tell you the same truth about what makes a proper swing, yet each has a unique style. Every musician will tell you what the right notes are for playing a particular piece, yet each will play the piece with a distinct flavor.

The moral life is similar. Each person practicing the virtue of patience practices it uniquely. Each couple aligning themselves with the nature of marriage practices the characteristics of marriage, such as fidelity and procreativity, uniquely.

The proper understanding of freedom is the predominant theme in *Veritatis Splendor,* making its appearance in nearly every article. The Pope terms the proper view of freedom "genuine freedom" (34), and here are some ways he expresses it:

"Freedom of conscience is never freedom 'from' the truth but always and only freedom 'in' the truth" (64).

"[According to certain erroneous opinions] human freedom would thus be able to 'create values' and would enjoy a primacy over truth, to the point that truth itself would be considered a creation of freedom. Freedom would thus lay claim to a *moral autonomy* which would actually amount to an *absolute sovereignty*" (35).

It is precisely this kind of "moral sovereignty" that God prohibited Adam and Eve from seizing in the garden. That's the meaning of the command not to eat of the tree of knowledge of—that is, *arbitership* over—good and evil (see *VS* 35).

See *VS:* 4; 16–18; 34–46; 61; 64. The theme of authentic freedom arises explicitly or implicitly throughout the entire text. Read *CCC:* 1730–48; 1733 concisely sums up the Christian view of freedom.

Do you think that the secular view of freedom—"I can do what I want so long as I don't hurt anyone else"—appears so attractive because it seems to let you have it both ways? It seems to promise that you can do what you want, yet at the same time showing great care for others.

Think about it—this claim is not a *viewpoint* at all but the lack (privation) of a viewpoint. For the moment a person voices it, he or she is caught in a contradiction. The claim begins by noting that "I can do whatever I want," and then quickly qualifies that: "I cannot harm anyone else."

So I *can't* do anything I want! I am bound by something true, namely, whatever would hurt another. Note that you can't get away from being bound to *some* version of the truth; the only remaining question is simply this: Where can you find the fullest understanding of the truth?

Or we can start with the second half of the secular position: "Don't hurt another." If I can do whatever I want, then it logically follows that *I* can decide what is harmful or not to someone else, and therefore the criterion "Don't hurt another" self-destructs. What if I think that it would be of great benefit to another person to surrender his or her freedom to my needs?[4] Think of Hitler.

If it is true that I can do as I want, then it must also be true that I can treat other people as I want. I may choose to stay within the bounds of civil law, but beyond that I can do as I please: "I'll do it my way."

There's another reason to challenge the proposition "I can do what I want so long as ..." Even if we do admit that there are certain actions that would harm others, how do we really know which acts are harmful and which aren't? And if an act is harmful, how do we measure the extent of such harm?

Murder obviously harms someone else. But do all so-called "private acts" harm no one? Where does one draw the supposed clear line between public and private acts? The word "harm" needs much clearer definition.

From even a purely human or natural standpoint, we see that our actions have far-reaching effects we ourselves don't always perceive. Meanwhile, our acts contribute to the *kind* of person we become, and it is *that person* who influences everyone with whom we come in contact. Ultimately everything that we do has ripple effects across the community. That's one reason we will face a universal "final judgment," when the full impact of our actions comes to light.

In sum, it is an illusion to think there is some large cross-section of action that "doesn't hurt anybody else." The secular view of freedom, then, is found wanting. The authentic view of freedom maintains that the human person is most free when knowing and living in accord with a higher, transcendent truth. Not only does such transcendence affect each individual, it affects whole cultures: "At the heart of every culture lies the attitude man takes to the greatest mystery: the mystery of God" (*CA* 24).

Looks like that settles the "freedom" part of the claim "I'm free to follow my conscience." What about the word *conscience*? If freedom means being aligned with truth, then what role is there for the conscience?

The truth is not something forced upon us. It is something God allows us to *discover*—we play an active role in this discovery. Conscience is the label given to that part of our being, centered in our intellect and will, that makes personal contact with transcendent truth.

Conscience is the medium between objective truth and our individual lives. For that reason, conscience can be called the "subjective norm" of the moral life. What is objectively true is also true *for us*, and what transcends all individuals is simultaneously a highly *personal* truth.[5]

Consider the words of Pope Pius XII:

The conscience is as it were the most secret and intimate cell man has. It is there that he takes refuge with spiritual faculties in absolute solitude: alone with himself, or better, alone with God—whose voice makes itself heard in the conscience—and with himself.... The conscience, therefore ... is a sanctuary, at whose threshold all must stop ... a jealously guarded shrine, whose secret God himself wishes to be preserved under the seal of the most sacred silence."[6]

The fathers of the Second Vatican Council quoted this text in *Gaudium et Spes* (16), and John Paul II uses it in *VS* (54).

Conscience allows a stunning combination of two truths that we often separate. The first truth is that we want to belong to something larger than ourselves. We see this desire clearly in Eastern religions, for example, which teach about a final happiness in which we get completely caught up in a final unity, so much so that we lose our individual uniqueness.

On the other hand, Westerners today tend to prize precisely that uniqueness, or individual*ity*. "I've gotta be me." This is the other truth so important to us.

In reality, these two truths converge: There is one Truth, from which all reality flows and to which all reality returns. Yet each individual embraces that Truth as something highly personal. We are simultaneously unique human persons who share a common human nature.[7] A very *friendly* reality, don't you think?

This stunning combination is a central theme of *VS*. Not only is it true that our uniqueness and freedom as individual persons are compatible with our having a common, universal human nature. It is also true that real or genuine freedom is found only when we align ourselves with this nature.

As article 51 of *VS* notes: "Universality does not ignore the individuality of human beings, nor is it opposed to the absolute uniqueness of each person. On the contrary, it embraces at its root each of the person's free acts, which are meant to bear witness to the universality of the true good."

Referring back to our analogies of the sportsman or the musician, we could say that their embrace of the right way to perform their skill is analogous to universality, while their ability to arrive at a unique golf swing or a unique rendering of a piece of music is analogous to conscience and individuality.

To introduce another analogy, consider the navigator and pilot of an airplane. You would never step foot on a plane unless you were confident that they were fully aligned with the truth about how to properly fly an airplane, and you relax knowing they have flown your route numerous times. At the same time, no two flights, even to the same destination, are exactly alike, as the navigator and pilot must apply their expertise in the nature of flying to an ensemble of particular conditions.

In this analogy, might the navigator represent universality and the pilot represent the unique application of the universal truth?

Good try, but both of them must grasp the universal truth, and both of them must know how to apply it. Even so, your instinct is partly right, in that they represent two aspects of the conscience at work: the intellect and the will.

The intellect is like the navigator who gets the lay of the land (or air), figures out what ought to be done, and tells the pilot what to do. The will is like the pilot who (we hope) aligns himself with the navigator and makes the airplane go where it is supposed to go. Either or both of them can err, and the analogy helps us to map out the complexities of the conscience.

Let's unravel a few distinctions: true and false conscience; good and bad conscience; vincible and invincible ignorance; and *malum* (or evil) and *culpa*, an evil for which one is culpable (see *VS* 81).

If you listen properly to the sources of truth, you have informed your conscience and are said to have a *true conscience*. A true conscience, then, is like a well-informed navigator. A *false* or *erroneous conscience* is one that has not been properly formed: The navigator errs.

Sometimes this error is not your fault. In that case, your false conscience is due to *invincible ignorance* (ignorance you are unable to conquer or overcome). For instance, someone who grows up in a heavily secularized atmosphere might not be fully responsible for certain immoral actions.

On the other hand, the ignorance could also be due to laziness or stubbornness, in which case you have actually *chosen* not to inform your conscience properly. Then, the ignorance is called *vincible* ("conquerable"), and you are culpable (worthy of blame) for the error.

Now for the pilot. When we use the phrase "following your conscience," we mean that your will does what your intellect tells it to do, whether the intellect is properly informed or not. This is analogous to the pilot's following the instruction of the navigator, whether the navigator's advice is accurate or not. Such a person is said to have a *good* conscience. On the other hand, the person who suffers from a *bad* conscience is one whose will does *not* follow the direction provided by the intellect.

Now we can combine the work of the navigator and the pilot and look at a full range of possibilities:

1. *A true and good conscience:* The navigator gets it right, and the pilot follows through. A good act results—the plane lands safely at its destination—and when the conscience is *habituated* to such good acts (makes a habit of them), truly virtuous acts ensue.

2. *A true but bad conscience:* The navigator gets it right, but the pilot fails to execute properly. The flight encounters unnecessary turbulence. This is one way that sin occurs. You *know* something to be evil (*malum*), yet you *act* contrary to that knowledge. Because you knew better, you are culpable (blameworthy) for having done the evil, and we speak of the act not only as a *malum* (an evil act) but a *culpa* (an evil act for which you are culpable).

3. *A false yet good conscience:* The navigator gets it wrong, and the pilot follows through on the wrong information. The result is a failed flight. If you have a false yet good conscience, are you *culpable* for the evil that has occurred? Let's reapply the distinction made just above, between invincible and vincible ignorance.

On the one hand, if there is no possible way that your intellect could have been properly informed, then we speak of your ignorance as *invincible*—unconquerable—and the evil is one for which you are not culpable. *Malum*, yes; *culpa*, no (see *VS* 62.1 and 63.1).

On the other hand, the navigator might have actually chosen the bad information given to the pilot. This could happen in two ways: He might know the truth and choose to repress it—bury it—because acknowledging it would be highly inconvenient (for example, the flight might last an extra couple hours if a wise detour is taken). Or he might have access to the truth and simply choose not to pursue it, knowing full well what the probable result of his inquiry would be.

Either way, the navigator (intellect) has willed his ignorance. Our common word for this is *rationalization.* If you do this in your conscience, you are culpable for the ensuing evil act. *Malum,* yes; *culpa,* yes.

We have discovered that not every evil (*malum*) involves guilt or a sin (*culpa*).[8] This insight is of incredible practical value. There are numerous people today who have come back to the Church after a damaging sojourn into subjectivism. They often return with an enormous amount of guilt. While some of that guilt may be very good, some might be false guilt due to the fact that they may have suffered from a fair amount of invincible ignorance.

Not uncommonly people were given bad advice about important moral matters, such as contraception or abortion. The ensuing ignorance may well be at least partially invincible, and while one should regret the evil done, the full weight of culpability is lifted. And even where culpability remains, total forgiveness is readily available.

4. One last category: *the false and bad conscience.* In this case the navigator, whether through vincible or invincible ignorance, gives false information to the pilot, and then the pilot, assuming this to be accurate information, nonetheless does not follow through on it. The irony of such a situation, rare as it may be, is that a good act may well ensue.

Imagine, for example, the committed atheist (with a malformed conscience) who thinks prayer rather silly, nonetheless saying his evening prayers (just to play it safe). As St. Thomas explains clearly, the will (pilot) is rejecting what is assumed to be true, and so the will is evil despite the goodness of the act.[9] *Malum*, no; *culpa*, yes.

These distinctions seem to have plenty of practical ramifications. Might the *malum/culpa* distinction help us deal with the accusation that we're being judgmental?

We are understandably afraid of being called "judgmental"— especially when Christ's saying "Judge not, that you be not judged" (Mt 7:1) is invoked—and we end up with what might be called the "can't impose syndrome": "I would never be able to justify having an abortion, but I can't impose my views on someone else." We might know how absurd such a claim is— substitute slave-holding for abortion, and it's pretty obvious— yet we don't want to be labeled as rigid and judgmental.

The solution is clear: We must steadfastly maintain the distinction between an act that is evil and an evil act for which someone is culpable. Christ demands that we make the former judgment, and prohibits us from making the latter judgment.

To judge that an act is right or wrong is precisely what conscience is supposed to do—in fact, the technical definition of conscience is that it is an "act of judgment" that applies the universal truth to a particular case (see *VS* 32.2 and 59.2). Judging that a particular individual is culpable for having committed an evil act is strictly forbidden—that's God's business.

Of course, I can accuse *myself* of culpability, which is precisely what would motivate me to seek reconciliation with God and neighbor.

By the way, once people properly understand conscience, the classic difficulty with the existence of hell (How could a good God send anyone to eternal damnation?) vanishes: Though in this life people can conveniently ignore the accusation of conscience, in the end they must listen, and then their own consciences make the ultimate accusation.

A proper understanding of conscience has another dramatic pastoral ramification. Today we often use the term "sincerity" to refer to a good conscience, and we often reduce "conscience" to mere sincerity, ignoring the existence of the true versus the erroneous conscience.[10] As a celebrity once said, "How can I be wrong when I'm so sincere?"[11]

To this we can respond: We appreciate your sincerity, but a sincere or good conscience does not make up for the fact that you have a falsely informed conscience. It would be better to say, "It's very easy to be wrong, and sincerity doesn't excuse. I must strive for a true conscience, and then act sincerely on that basis."

In *VS* 32, the pope criticizes the tendency to reduce the true conscience to the sincere (good) conscience:

> To the affirmation that one has a duty to follow one's conscience is unduly added the affirmation that one's moral judgment is true merely by the fact that it has its origin in the conscience. But in this way the inescapable claims of truth disappear, yielding their place to a criterion of sincerity, authenticity, and "Being at peace with

oneself," so much so that some have come to adopt a radically subjectivistic conception of moral judgment.

Earlier we defined conscience as a judgment. The pope notes how important this word is, because it connotes that we are placing our actions against the backdrop of objective truth. In *VS* 55, he notes how some contemporary authors err in using the term "decision" rather than judgment. Conscience does more than merely *decide;* it *judges*—that is, it evaluates according to standards.

Read *VS:* 54–64.
Study *CCC:* 1776–94.

I'm curious about the case of the true but bad conscience (second question). Is it really possible to know the truth and yet freely act contrary to it? Most people really try to do what is good; it's just that they don't always *know* what the good is.

But now I see I've gotten myself into a dilemma, because that would make sin impossible: All people would be excused from their bad acts because they were ignorant of the good and they meant well.

You've hit upon the classical pagan view of intellect and will. For Plato, if you truly know the good, you will do it. Likewise, if you don't do the good, it must be because you didn't fully know the good.

As you say, this analysis seems to correspond with a common experience. Sometimes when we do something that we later reflect upon as wrong, we tend to say, "I didn't really know it was wrong." Had we fully understood the wrongness of the act, of course we would not have done it. But we did not fully understand, due to all sorts of factors beyond our control.

From this comes the dilemma in which you find yourself: It must be true either that people don't generally try to do good, or else that people never sin. Congratulations, by the way— most people don't like to admit that they've been caught in a dilemma!

Try this interactive game. First, look at the two horns of the dilemma you think you are in, between which you must choose:

1. You want to admit that sin exists, and so you want to assert that people really do *choose evil*. But then you seem to have a rather low or depraved view of humankind.

2. You want to focus on humankind as good, but then you can't hang on to the reality of sin.

Next, consider two historical movements: Secularism and certain forms of Reformation thought. Now match each historical movement with one or the other horns of the dilemma.

Secularism tries to dissolve the dilemma by ignoring horn 1. It claims that there's no sin, everyone is good, and bad things are caused by bad social arrangements. It focuses on horn 2: People are seen as essentially good, and sin is eliminated.

On the other hand, certain forms of Reformation theology try to dissolve the dilemma by ignoring horn 2 and focusing on horn 1: People aren't good; they are sinful in their very essence.

The former approach captures something about humanity's inherent goodness; the latter captures something about humanity's inherent sinfulness. And in this dilemma, you feel as if you have to choose one or the other.

I have good news for you! You don't have to choose either one, and at the same time you can appreciate the profound insight that lies within each one. As a Catholic you can solve the dilemma without dissolving either horn! And you can see your friends who may think this way not as *wrong* so much as *partially right.*

Are you some kind of magician? Show me how you can solve this dilemma!

God is the one who pulls off this trick—and you'll see that it's not tricky at all. First, let's replay the dilemma with two important historical figures. St. Paul felt the dilemma profoundly: "I do not understand my own actions. For I do not do what I want, but I do the very thing I hate" (Rom 7:15). He was aware that sin exists, but also aware that sin doesn't quite make sense given that we really want to do good.

St. Augustine likewise struggled with this dilemma in his autobiography, *The Confessions,* as he reflected upon his adolescent experience of stealing pears with a group of friends.[12] He tried to discern why he did this. The pears were not particularly tasty; he was not hungry; there was no profit to be made from them.

Augustine seemed unable to ascertain any purpose toward which he had acted. How could his intellect know the good, and his will nevertheless freely choose to act against it? Just as you said in your question, we don't go around intentionally seeking evil.

On the other hand, we do catch ourselves sinning. Since we are decent people who want to do good, we often have a ready excuse at hand, usually something like "I didn't really mean to do it." In other words, I think I sinned, but no, it's not really a sin because I wasn't planning on doing something evil.

In fact, we are repulsed by the very word "evil"—that's just something we don't do! Maybe Hitler or bin Laden did evil, but *me?* No way.

What happened to Augustine is that he "caught himself" doing an evil (however minor) for which he just could not find *any* excuse—and it shocked him. Augustine asked, terrified, "Can one unravel this twisted tangle of knots? I shudder to look at it or think of such abomination" (II, 10).

Let's get St. Thomas Aquinas to help us straighten all this out. According to his reasoning, Augustine did not choose to steal the pears because it was evil. He did it because he wanted *some good.* As St. Thomas teaches, all actions are done *under the aspect of the good,* that is, because the act *appears to us as good.*

For Augustine, perhaps this was the good of exercising his own will—very much a part of life for most adolescents (and plenty of adults, too!) His intellect simultaneously knew that it was evil to steal the pears, just as adolescents know that it's wrong to be unkind to their parents and siblings. But Augustine, like most adolescents, was engaged in a battle.

Exercising his will, in and of itself, is of course a great good. Exercising his will *in a way contrary to the moral law* (stealing) is pursuing a good in a disordered way. He allowed his desire for that good—exercising his will—to "win out" over the true good his intellect knew.

Call it the battle of the goods! The true, the good, and the beautiful are so powerful that people cannot rid themselves of them—they sneak in from behind, as it were, even in our attempt to dismiss them. All our actions are done under the aspect of the good. St. Thomas calls this the "first principle in the practical reason."

Now, once we realize that we inevitably seek good, we want to be sure that we pursue the true good, the properly ordered good, and avoid evil—that is, disordered goods (goods "out of order"), or privations (lack) of rightly ordered goods. We naturally say to ourselves "good is to be done and pursued, and evil is to be avoided." In short, "do good and avoid evil."

That we seek the true good is of course no guarantee that we will find the true good. It's all too easy to seek disordered goods—there's the "battle of the goods." Nevertheless, we all seek the good, even the most hardened criminals. There is even a fancy name—*synderesis*—that the Catholic moral tradition gives to this habit by which we are wedded to the good. *Synderesis* is what makes us aim at the good and avoid evil, "incite to good and murmur at evil."[13]

This is *very* exciting—but could you provide more examples, please!

Coming right up. The item you steal might help you accomplish something worthwhile. The pleasure you take in an impure thought or impure act is a good in and of itself, but in these instances is taken illicitly. If you are a student, you may have fun watching a great basketball game on TV, but at a time when studying for an exam should be top priority. You enjoy a fine piece of chocolate cake, but at a time when dieting is of critical importance.

If all those things weren't goods in themselves, people doing such acts wouldn't act in the first place! In each of these examples, although a good is being pursued, it is not a properly ordered good. When placed in context of our ultimate destiny (union with God, salvation) we see that these goods were pursued at the wrong time (sex before marriage), or with the wrong person (adultery), or in the wrong way (theft to get money for something truly good), or in the wrong place (people-watching during Mass), or in the wrong manner (plagiarism).

In each instance the good pursued was *out of order*. We use the expression, when someone does something shabby, "That was low." The person ought to *order* the good properly—obtain the item fairly, not through theft, and take pleasure in good acts, not sinful ones.

Not to do so is a disordered or *inordinate* act, an act *incommensurate* with—not "measured" under—the highest good.[14] It wasn't headed the right direction. The "end of the act" (*finis operis,* if you like the Latin) was thwarted.

When a good is chosen that is not in proper alignment with the highest good, with God's will, then the ordering that ought to be present isn't present. Put another way, a *privation* takes place.

Imagine atomic power not directed toward *fueling* a city, but toward *blowing up* a city. The power is in itself a good thing, but it is not ordered properly. Talk about a privation!

Or think about the water running out of a spigot, properly directed. When some part in the spigot wears out or is missing, the water sprays every which way. When it does, you sure experience the lack, the privation, of due order!

So, too, with our moral actions. Actions not ordered under the highest good—inordinate actions—prevent the good that ought to be present. *A part of the universe that could have come into existence is kept from coming into existence.* As Thomas noted, "good and being are convertible."[15]

What he means is this: When we do the good, we create more order (good) and hence more being in the universe. On the other hand, when we sin, when we choose disorder, we prevent that being. The evil we choose is thus a *privation*—a loss.

Our capacity to effect being itself, by our actions, is at once frightening—due to the responsibility it entails—and awesome—due to the dignity it allows man. We can place this insight into the even richer context of Christ's grace. Christ himself appears in our moral acts—each act is an expression of Christ's grace and a participation in God's creative power. There is a *sacramental structure* to human action, such that grace *appears in history* through our moral acts, just as the sacraments are both signs and causes of grace.[16]

Looks like I've found the solution to the common query "How can it be wrong when it feels so good?" You're saying that wrong acts have some good in them, and that their wrongness comes from the lack of due order. Does that lack of due order wreck other goods, too?

Sin is the choice of a good that is not integrated properly in light of the highest good. It's a "spoiled" good.[17] Since it has "fallen out" of order, we could call it a lesser good, a disjointed good, or better, a "lower-than-it-ought-to-be" good.

There may be some good, for example, in the act of theft (the enjoyment of the item stolen). But that good of enjoyment has been gained in a disordered way—it has fallen out of its due order. To be properly aligned under the highest good, it must position itself in harmony with another good: respect for another's property. Through theft, that great good has been lost!

Take another example: Sexual pleasure is a good that is an expression of marital commitment. When that pleasure, good in and of itself, is sought outside marriage, the good it ought to be expressing—permanent commitment—is missing. So you're absolutely right: the pursuit of a "lower-than-it-ought-to-be good," or a "good out of proper order," wrecks those other goods with which it should be in proper alignment.

In these two examples, respect for property or for marital commitment is now absent. Sin, then, is an act *lacking* order that a person has freely chosen. And that lack of order causes the absence of the higher good that ought to be there but isn't. Sin is thus the *privation of a due good*.[18]

One more step. Remember that the ultimate ordering principle is our final end, God himself. So what happens when we throw goods out of order? Well, we can't get rid of God, the ultimate ordering principle. So instead we refuse to acknowledge him as the ultimate ordering principle.[19]

We should be participating in the order God provides, but we decide not to do so. It is in this sense, then, that sin involves

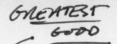

GREATEST
GOOD

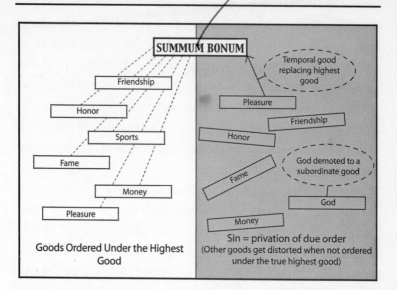

SUMMUM BONUM

Friendship
Honor
Sports
Fame
Money
Pleasure

Goods Ordered Under the Highest Good

Temporal good replacing highest good

Pleasure
Friendship
Honor
Fame
Money

God demoted to a subordinate good

God

Sin = privation of due order
(Other goods get distorted when not ordered under the true highest good)

idolatry: placing some created good in the place of God. And since we are the ones placing something else in the place of the highest good, in sinful acts we are loving ourselves more than God.[20] Back to Augustine's experience: He was loving the exercise of his own will, out of order, and so loving himself more than God.

With this understanding of conscience, sin, and human acts, it should be clear that the moral life does not involve sifting through a set of external regulations, finding what is absolutely forbidden and what we can get away with—a crude, arbitrary game set up by a god whose main goal is to take most of the fun out of life. The moral life is rather about living the *good* life, reaping the incredible benefits of *participating* in the goods ordered under the highest good (known as *theonomy*). Only goods thus ordered can truly satisfy.

The first chapter of *VS* (6–27) is an interpretation of the parable of the rich young man. The interpretation is cast in terms of God, who is our origin and destiny, calling each of us. Note especially the beginning of art. 12: "Only God can answer the question about the good, because he is the Good. But God has already given an answer to this question; he did so *by creating man and ordering him* with wisdom and love to his final end, through the law which is inscribed on his heart (see Rom 2:15), the 'natural law.'"

We participate in God's ordering Wisdom. Each unique individual comes from a common source—the Creator—and is called to a common final end, an end that will not destroy our uniqueness but rather be the perfection of it. Living the moral life means being on the trajectory toward that ultimate end.

What a far cry from a rigid moral*ism* that reduces the moral life to a stringent list of do's and don'ts! The absolute moral norms that play a critically important role in the good life are placed in so much broader a context: The moral life is a participation in our ultimate destiny.

And guess what? That eternal destiny, union with God himself, *is already present in the here and now,* in our very hearts. As a favorite prayer says, "God, make my soul your heaven." We really do *participate* in the *ordering principle* of our lives, and that principle is actually a Person, a personal God. In the next chapter we'll say a lot more about the sheer beauty of our own *participation* in the order that comes from God.

TWO

TRUTH IS FRIENDLY TO US: THE MEANING OF PARTICIPATED THEONOMY

The perspective you suggest is refreshing—too often we reduce the moral life to a list of do's and don'ts. On the other hand, it's really important to talk about sin, in an age beset by moral relativism, which has wrought unfathomable damage on individuals, families, and society at large. Doesn't it seem pretty clear that we need a return to the clear rules of "the good old days"?

You're correct about the ravages of moral relativism—what we might call moral *autonomy*, in which each person is a law unto himself or herself. But it may not be too wise to return to a neat and tidy past (which wasn't quite as neat and tidy as we'd like to think).

Imagine a person immersed in moral autonomy. He has become his own god, arbitrating over moral good and evil. Eventually he hits rock bottom—he becomes a slave to his passions—and begins to see the emptiness of moral autonomy.

What is his natural tendency? He wants to get as far away from his past experience as possible, and so reverts to what *VS* calls *heteronomy*—a system in which moral truth is solid as can be, but is surrounded by a cult-like harshness and rigidity in which the person is ruled by someone or something else. That might initially look attractive because there is no room for the individual self—the thing that led the person into moral autonomy in the first place.

If *autonomy* means "self-law," *heteronomy* means an "alien law," a truth that is alien to the individual person. Seeing Christianity as a heteronomous system means we say: "I believe the truth because someone *else* told me it was true." "Do it because I told you to do it."

In this approach, the truth is extrinsically imposed on the individual (that is, imposed from the outside), violating the dignity of the person. What is our reaction to truth that is extrinsically imposed, but ignores our individuality? We want to keep our distance from it—and the tendency is to revert right back toward moral autonomy or relativism (individual*ism*).

The Church's moral vision avoids the extremes of both autonomy and heteronomy. It avoids the individual*ism* of moral autonomy, but retains the proper individual*ity* that heteronomy tends to deny. There really is a moral truth that we can know and live, but it is a truth that resonates with the core of our being, a truth that genuinely "sets us free" (see Jn 8:32). It's freedom *for* the truth, not freedom *from* the truth, which is not true freedom, but license.

Instead of the truth being true simply "because God commanded it," it's just the reverse: God commanded it *because it is true.* We might say that the truth is *friendly* to our being. It affirms our unique individual*ity* while helping us to avoid that enslaving focus on the individual called individual*ism.*

We accept the truth because it is true; it is built *for us.* And we respect the authority behind the truth—God, the Church, Scripture, the Magisterium—because that authority is in the service of the truth. "The truth can impose itself on us only by virtue of its own truth."[1] We act in accord with the Truth because in a sense it is *our* truth, and *we* recognize, acknowledge, accept it as true.

Now please prepare yourself for a key idea that will resonate throughout the rest of the book—and it's not just an idea, but a truth that can resonate throughout your whole life. The name of the morality that avoids both autonomy and heteronomy is *participated theonomy* (*VS* 41). Don't be afraid of a couple of big words! *Participated theonomy* is a fancy way of saying that God's truth is built *for us*—his moral law (theonomy) is something we really participate or partake in.[2]

The notion of "participation" is easier to understand if we consider another aspect of the Christian life: God's grace dwelling in us. It has "twin" aspects: First, sanctifying grace is not a *thing* we have in our souls, but is the very life of the Triune God dwelling—pulsating, if you will—within our very being. Grace is God's love poured into our hearts (see Rom 5:5).

Second, looked at from our angle, when God pours himself into us, we *participate* in him (See *VS* 73, and *CCC* 1709, 1987–2016). And part of God's being is his law—not a set of rules only, as a heteronomy would have it, but the whole set of principles that puts our moral lives in order.

Twin moments again: When God pours himself into us, he pours that "order" into us. (Later we'll see that this is precisely what the "natural law" is.) From our angle, we partake in that order. It is there *for* our happiness.

That's what participated theonomy is. When you see this term throughout the book, think "God's truth is friendly to *me*," or "God's truth is meant to make me *truly* happy." That's participated theonomy in a nutshell.

This way of looking at things—participated theonomy as the mid-point between the extremes of autonomy and heteronomy—seems extremely helpful for understanding all sorts of things about the moral life. It's theoretical, but it has a *practical* value—that's my type of theory!

We've already seen one benefit: It helps us understand why people mired in autonomy so easily can fly straight into the (unloving) arms of heteronomy, and how those who grow up squelched by heteronomy fly straight into the supposedly "freeing" arms of autonomy (which doesn't free a person at all).

Here is another "pastoral aid" that this understanding yields: When you embrace the Church's moral stance of participated theonomy, expect to be misunderstood by people on both of the opposite extremes. Those who are positioned within autonomy will look at participated theonomy and see it as heteronomous. Because you claim, with the Church, to have access to truths that are absolute in nature, you'll be caricatured as an intolerant rigid fundamentalist who wants to impose one opinion on everyone.

On the other hand, those who are positioned heteronomously will look at participated theonomy as far too autonomous for their tastes. Because you claim, with the Church, that the solution to our current moral crisis is not a return to the pre-Vatican II past, you'll be caricatured as a loose, wimpy Catholic without any real moral fiber.

In the midst of these two misunderstandings, be patient and non-polemical.[3] Take some comfort in knowing that when you are misunderstood by two polar opposites, that's a good sign that you're getting something right!

Is "participated theonomy" a brand new concept? What else does it involve?

Since it essentially means that the moral life is *following Christ*, it is as old as Christianity. In fact, it is as old as creation, as we shall soon see. But in another sense it looks new to us because for the last four hundred years or so Catholic moral theology, in noble attempts to respond to new historical situations such as the Reformation and the Enlightenment, lost sight of some of its best insights.

For instance, the Enlightenment focused upon the importance of human reason. Much of moral theology responded in kind, showing that the Christian moral life could be understood using purely rational and philosophical categories. The result is often called the "manualist" tradition, named after the highly systematic manuals used in seminary formation.

Using the categories learned above, we might say that the Church responded to the dangers of moral *autonomy* (part of the heritage of the Enlightenment) with a firm, rational approach that today appears as somewhat *heteronomous*. An important insight here: That approach may well have been appropriate in its own context. Only when we try to retrieve that approach in a new historical setting does it appear stultified and heteronomous.

The Second Vatican Council was a brilliant moment for the Church, retrieving many riches from her tradition that had been obscured, and applying those riches in a new historical setting. Of course, the implementation of the Council was not always quite so brilliant; the documents were misused by many who saw an opportunity to advance a more autonomous view of reality. Many Catholics understandably reacted with a heteronomous swing to the past—the Society of St. Pius X founded by Marcel Lefebvre is a case in point.

Originally there was to have been a document on moral theology at the Second Vatican Council. The early drafts, however, tended to use the same methodology found in the traditional "manuals" of moral theology. They failed to situate the moral life *Christocentrically* (that is, with Christ at the center).[4] And so, the project was put off for the future, with only a simple directive that attention should be given to a more scripturally based moral theology.[5] The encyclical *Veritatis Splendor*, with hundreds of biblical references, is the long-awaited document that never came to fruition at Vatican II.

We can enumerate four key themes of participated theonomy that radiate throughout the encyclical (please see the web site for *all* the key *VS* texts):

1. *The call to holiness—toward our Final End.* Participated theonomy places all the individual elements of the moral life—sin, virtue, dilemmas, hard cases—in the much broader spectrum of each person's *journey* toward the ultimate end: complete happiness with God, the beatific vision. This larger vision prevents the nitty-gritty elements of the moral life—such as figuring out whether a sin is mortal or venial—from becoming ends in themselves. Those elements are important, but only insofar as they contribute to the larger picture: living our whole life in a way compatible with our final end.

Placing the moral life on this trajectory is called *teleological* ethics (from the Greek word for "end" or "goal," *telos*). When our whole life is on this trajectory, we are pursuing the *call to holiness,* a call central to every Christian's life. Because the call to holiness includes a call to virtuous living, our focus on our final end simultaneously allows us to contribute to the "earthly city"—one of the central tenets of Catholic social teaching.

2. *The person of Jesus Christ.* Participated theonomy emphasizes that the moral journey toward the ultimate end is accomplished by walking with a Person, the person of Jesus Christ. So participated theonomy is thoroughly *Christocentric.*

VS begins with the parable of the rich young man who walked away sadly when Christ asked him to abandon himself completely. The young man had part of the moral life down cold: He never broke any of the absolute norms found in the Ten Commandments. But the moral life is so much more than following the rules.

Important as they are, an exclusive focus upon the rules leads to a heteronomous view, just as relativizing them leads to an autonomous view. The moral norms are but one component of living with Christ. They are a set of absolute ground rules that set the stage for something spectacular: a personal relationship with Christ.

3. *The life of grace.* The personal relationship with Christ so central to participated theonomy is unlike any other personal relationship we experience, no matter how intimate. For by means of our relationship with Christ, God pours his very being into our being. This is the gift of the Holy Spirit, also called *sanctifying grace.*

Looked at from our side, we become partakers or sharers in the divine life. Making this observation is precisely how *VS* meets the request of Vatican II for a more scripturally based morality. Consider, for example, the following biblical texts, searching for the key vocabulary used to describe grace, our participation in the divine life: 1 Jn 3; 2 Cor 3:18; 5:16-21; Gal 4:5-7; 6:15; Eph 2:18-19; 2 Pt 1:3-5.

The indwelling of the Spirit, then, assists us in living the moral life, or to put it more bluntly, *enables* us to live the moral life—for without grace we can do nothing. The gifts of the Holy Spirit assist us in developing a life of *virtue* as an integral part of our call to holiness. (In our later discussion of the virtues, we will speak of the *infused-by-grace moral virtues*).

4. *The Trinity*. If you look back over the last three points, what central Christian dogma comes to mind? Participated theonomy is structured according to the "logic" of the Trinity. We are created by the Father and are headed toward him. "In our end is our beginning," as T.S. Eliot put it; this theme of "going forth and returning" is often referred to using the Latin *exitus et reditus*.

We are not on our own. Christ is beside us all the way. And the Spirit dwells in our very being. The Trinity, far from being an abstract dogma in the realm of unintelligible mystery, is rather a transcendent mystery that is right in our midst and highly pertinent to our moral and spiritual lives.

The Trinitarian mystery infuses Scripture—hidden in the Old Testament, explicit in the New. The Council fathers asked for just the right thing when they requested a renewal of moral theology with greater attention to Scripture. As you read *VS* alongside this book, watch for the numerous scriptural references—there are well over three hundred!

The manualist tradition erred precisely in failing to integrate ethics with Scripture and into the other great mysteries of the Christian faith. It also made the mistake of *imposing* the rules of ethics rather than allowing a *discovery* of the truth. Many priests and theologians were trained under the heteronomous manualist methods, and it's sad but no surprise that they reacted as they did: They fell into an autonomous view of the moral life and dissented from Catholic moral teaching. When the Catholic faithful and they themselves were besieged by the moral relativism of a secular age, the tried and true moral rules cracked under the pressure—for those rules were not integrated properly into the full texture of the Trinitarian Christian life.

The "teleological" idea—that the moral life means living on a trajectory toward our ultimate heavenly end—is wonderful. But how do you answer those who want to put all their energy into improving the world? They tend either to abandon Christianity as a "pie in the sky" fantasy, or else to turn Christianity into a social reform program, focusing on a redistribution of worldly goods.

It is essential to grasp the Christian conception of history, found in Scripture and tradition, and heavily influenced by St. Augustine's understanding as put forth in his classic work *The City of God:* Certainly all humans live within history. But the best way to improve the world is by an awareness—a membership in—another "city" or "kingdom" far more important: the kingdom of God or the city of God.

Those who follow Christ and have grace in their hearts are citizens of this city—and as we'll see later, non-Christians can have some connection to this city. (The "charter" of this city is the beatitudes—see *CCC* 1716–24.) Members of the Church, then, have a dual citizenship, in both the city of God and in the historical, political order. As *Gaudium et Spes* 43 notes: "This council exhorts Christians, as citizens of two cities, to strive to discharge their earthly duties conscientiously and in response to the Gospel spirit."

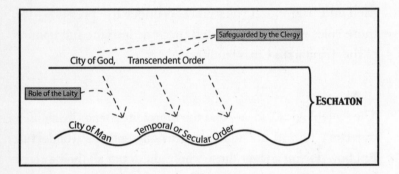

The wavy line in this diagram represents temporal history with all its ups and downs. The thick, solid line represents the solidity of the kingdom of God. The two lines are separate yet related. They are separate because human history can never "become" the kingdom of God: There can be no earthly utopia. They are related because citizens of the kingdom live within human history and can influence that history. Such influence is represented by the arrows, which connect the kingdom of God to temporal history without identifying the two.

The Church has a saving and eschatological purpose which can be fully attained only in the future world. But she is already present in this world, and is composed of men, that is, members of the earthly city who have a call to form the family of God's children during the present history of the human race, and to keep increasing it until the Lord returns (*GS* 40).

It is absolutely obligatory for the Christian to live within history and to bring the light of the Gospel to bear on history: "Therefore let there be no opposition between professional and social activities on the one part, and religious life on the other.... The Christian who neglects his temporal duties ... jeopardizes his eternal salvation" (*GS* 43).

For instance, a Christian living virtuously will have an effect on human history, and numerous Christians living virtuously will have a massive effect. The arrows in the diagram are precisely what the more concrete aspects of Catholic social thought are all about: guidelines as to how virtuous human beings ought to act in history in such a way as to improve the human condition.

I noticed the *eschaton* in the diagram. What exactly is it? I know it has something to do with the end of the world, but does the eschaton have any concrete impact on my life here and now?

God himself will be the One who one day brings about the eschaton, a "new heavens and a new earth." The eschaton is the end of the world *as we know it.* Though it might seem to be pretty far removed from our daily lives, it actually has profound ramifications for how we live and act in society.[6]

The future eschaton reminds us that the best way to improve society is first to realize that a utopia cannot be had—in fact, that's a sure way to make conditions even worse. Only God can bring about a utopia, and this occurs eschatologically (that is, at the end). Here on earth our highest liberation comes first from our membership in the City of God, giving us the "freedom of the sons of God," or grace.

In anticipating the eschaton, then, we can actually make it partially present—much as a child dreaming of Christmas months ahead of time actually experiences a bit of Christmas. In following God's will and living virtuously, we improve society.

As Christians, with this eschatological sense, we ought to do our *best* at improving society because, having given all to God, we have nothing to lose. We live in the world and care for the world but are detached from the world. That means we're really free—we can be bold and daring in our concern for others and concern for society, no matter the cost.

Precisely because we are members of the transcendent city of God, the kingdom of heaven, we are *energized* to live the authentically good moral life. It is highly energizing—not to mention a great relief—to realize that we need not figure out the truth about reality, the truth about the good life, all on our own. There is an order, God's order (theonomy), in which we can participate.

A great relief, and a great challenge! It seems that two seemingly opposite ideas are both absolutely essential and compatible with one another: Improve the world, and live for heaven! Is this what the distinctive role of the laity is all about?

Exactly (see *LG* 31). The layperson's *vocation* involves three interrelated aspects. First is the baptismal vocation, the call to sanctity (see *VS* 107.2). Second is one's state in life, either married or celibate (as distinct from the vocation to the priesthood or to a religious order).

Third is the vocation to reflect the truths of the faith in the secular order. This means to live as a virtuous person in the secular world, and it also means to follow, when applicable, the principles of Catholic social thought (to be discussed later) in the political, economic, or cultural sphere. The term *apostolate* is used to indicate a specific kind of activity in the temporal order. For instance, a businessman has the apostolate of bringing the truths of the gospel into his particular sphere of expertise.

When Christians shine the light of the gospel onto the temporal order, they ask whether this or that aspect of the temporal order is *compatible* with the Gospel. If so, no problem. If there is incompatibility, then a serious problem exists; it is to be challenged, using prudent means, by the Christian layperson.

If a form of entertainment displays vulgar language, racism, or sexism, it is incompatible with the gospel and ought to be challenged. MD's who abort babies must be challenged. If a business is treating customers unfairly, its policy is incompatible with the gospel and should be challenged. So, too, with an educational system that promotes promiscuity, or slips various forms of relativism into the classroom. The same with a psychological theory—and practice—that is relativistic and seeks only to help clients feel more comfortable with themselves (that is, more comfortable with—feeling less guilty about—sin).

The Church is an "expert in humanity" (*SRS* 7).[7] She is not an expert in business, science, engineering, education, or any other temporal affair. She is an expert in what it means to be a human person and is capable of discerning what is out of alignment with human nature.

For that reason, she has no particular temporal mission, yet at the same time she is concerned with all temporal affairs (See *GS* 42). Christianity is not to be understood as a *means* to some other good, such as a more just social order.[8] Christianity is an end in itself.

Put otherwise, the call to "put on Christ" through the sacraments is an end in itself. A marvelous side-effect of people pursuing this end is a more just social order, and if a great many people of a nation pursue this end, their society will be a supremely just place in which to live. Due to sin, however, such bettering of society is very imperfect.

The moral life is all about individuals practicing virtue and growing in sanctity and thereby sanctifying the world. The Church may never be involved in partisan politics, and the leaders of the Church may never take public office, because the Church is not a social reform agency but a "sin reform" body. The clergy exist first and foremost to invite individuals to live a sacramental life, leading to sanctity.

It seems that since Vatican II we've had exactly the opposite of what Vatican II taught—lots of clergy are interested in the tasks of laypeople, and lots of laity want to do clerical activities. Do you think that's true?

Ironically, while the laity became more involved in Church-related affairs (the clericalization of the laity), the clergy began to see as their own duty what was traditionally the laity's (the laicization of the clergy). And then, both roles were devalued.[9] Rather than imposing on the laity—and on the world—any particular political agenda, it is the duty of the clergy tirelessly to preach the gospel, inviting all to become ever more vital members of the Church of Christ, the kingdom of God here on earth. The truths of the faith and the truths of the moral life must be preached and taught.

Among the truths of the moral life are found certain social principles—the body of Catholic social thought. It is the duty of the laity to live as Christians in the social sphere and bring the principles of social thought to bear on social life. One of the most important of such principles is the natural law—the subject of our next chapter.

THREE

"How Can It Be Wrong When It Feels So Good?": The Natural Law

We've now seen the proper meaning of the phrase "I am free to follow my conscience." Freedom means being aligned with the truth. Conscience must be informed by that truth. And it is the unique task of the laity to bring that truth into the temporal order. The million-dollar question, then, is this: How do I inform myself of the truth?

A rather important question, as many think there is *no answer to it.* Actually, those who think this way actually propose an answer: autonomy. They themselves are the source of truth.

It's more humble and realistic, however, to look outside ourselves for the truth, to something eternal. St. Thomas calls the total sum of truth, existing in God, the "eternal law."

We participate in this truth—it is poured into us—in two ways. A portion of that truth has been *revealed* to us, and this portion is called the *divine law.* It's the topic of chapter five.

The other portion of the truth is planted in our nature in such a way that we grasp it *naturally*, almost as if by instinct— we can't *not* know it—and we can use human reason to arrive at it and articulate it.[1] It is not imposed heteronomously—it speaks from within (participated theonomy).

Finally, human law (civil or ecclesiastical law) should be based on the natural law, but cannot include the entirety of the natural law. St. Thomas' *Treatise on Law* is the classic source for these four types, and Pope John Paul II refers to it a number of times in *VS*.[2]

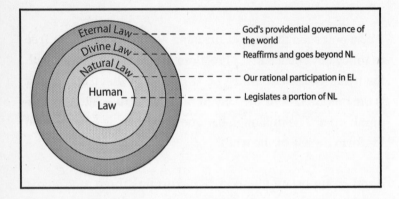

The natural law is that portion of the truth St. Paul seizes upon in his letter to the Romans, speaking of those who have not come in contact with God's specific revelation in the Judeo-Christian tradition. Are they responsible for their irreligiosity and moral perversity?

When Gentiles who have not the law do by nature what the law requires, they are a law to themselves, even though they do not have the law. They show that what the law requires is written on their hearts, while their conscience also bears witness and their conflicting thoughts accuse or perhaps excuse them on that day when .... God judges the secrets of men by Christ Jesus.

ROMANS 2:14-16 (also see ROMANS 1:19-20)

Just as there are certain physical laws of the universe discernible through reason, so too with moral truths. These are truths that *we cannot not know*.[3] Natural law is that portion of the eternal law planted in us by nature, or put otherwise, it is our participation in the eternal law.[4]

Read *CCC:* 1954–74.

Don't you think that the very word "law" rubs us the wrong way, appearing as arbitrary and heteronomous—like the unfair traffic ticket? And isn't it the same with the word "reason"? We think of "cold, calculating reason," so rigorously logical that it is insensitive to the real lives of individuals.

You're right, but let's use that phenomenon as a positive opportunity. Just because something is misunderstood and misused is no reason to abandon it. Misuse does not nullify proper use.

Religion itself is a prime example of this principle. It often has been horribly abused. ("The devil can cite Scripture for his purpose.") Sometimes, in fact, the degree to which a thing is misused is an indicator of how valuable it is!

Since we are multiplying famous sayings, let's add this one: "The corruption of the best is the worst." Authentic religion is the most important thing in the world—the Trinitarian life dwelling within us. But when religion is corrupted, prepare for the worst.

Now, back to *law*. We've all had unfortunate experiences in which we were treated unfairly due to some arbitrary law. But the *natural* law fits perfectly with participated theonomy—it is made for us, placed in our being; we participate in it.

John Paul II emphasizes this point: "He cares for man not 'from without,' through the laws of physical nature, but 'from within,' through reason, which, by its natural knowledge of God's eternal law, is consequently able to show man the right direction to take in his free actions."[5] As we'll see momentarily, when civil laws are designed in harmony with the natural law, they, too, can be friendly to us.

Now to the word *reason*. When seen as something cold and imposing, it is misused in the direction of heteronomy. As for the autonomous misuse, we have just the right word: rationalization. Participated theonomy rescues reason from both these abuses.

Remember the "battle of the goods" in chapter one? Because of original sin and the resulting concupiscence (weakness), it is so easy to get the goods of life out of alignment. Lower goods aren't ordered under higher goods, and created goods compete with the highest good. The result is a privation of due order, and the effects are devastating.

Recall the example of the faulty water spigot. The wonderful ordered flow of water is severely disordered, and that disordered good wreaks havoc all over the place. We can't get upset over the water itself, but rather over the disordered flow of the water (the corruption of the best is the worst).

We don't tell the plumber, "Cut off that nasty water for good!" but rather "Get that water to flow properly!" And what a delight to get it fixed!

Reason is precisely what allows us to get all the goods of human life in proper order. Thomas says "the rule and measure of human acts is reason ... since it belongs to reason to direct to the end."[6] Reason allows us to *participate* in the right order of things that occurs with *theonomy*—the ordering of all goods *under God*, the highest good.

It looks like participated theonomy has a rational component. I have a friend at work who loves to get into philosophical discussions (he's a bit of a relativist), and he tells me that my arguments are just based on faith. Is natural law the tool I'm looking for?

Natural law is that portion of the eternal law that is accessible to any reasonable person. So it's just what you need—your friend will no longer be able conveniently to dismiss your arguments as "religious." And natural law is precisely the tool so desperately needed by the laity to speak about transcendent truth in the "public square" of our nation's life (see *VS* 97.2, and 98–101).

Now more than ever, our nation needs the truths of the natural law. Since Catholics are (or should be) particularly skilled "natural lawyers," this is a special moment for Catholics. It is a real "Catholic moment."

Imagine the reaction if you were to use a religiously based argument to defend the dignity of the unborn about to be aborted or the handicapped or elderly about to be euthanized. A typical response from an opponent would be that your arguments are based in your religion, and in our political order you may not force your religion on others; all are granted religious freedom. Put most bluntly: "If you don't believe abortion is right, don't have one," or "If you don't believe in homosexual marriage, don't marry a homosexual."

For this reason, it is very important to be able to establish the truth about human dignity on the basis of reason alone. We must be able to appeal to the natural moral law that is inscribed in our being simply by virtue of the fact that we are human beings, rather than appealing first and foremost to the divine revealed law. We must insist that our civil laws should always be compatible with the natural law. They should never contradict the natural law.

In fact, only a clear understanding of the natural law allows us to make any sense out of our nation's founding principles.[7] The Declaration of Independence refers to "nature and nature's God." Precisely because there is a transcendent God on whom we are dependent ("In God we trust"), our rights to life, liberty, and the pursuit of happiness cannot be seized by a tyrant—they are *inalienable.*

The government, rather, must *serve* the citizenry and *assist,* rather than stifle their numerous organizations and associations—churches, schools, families, and many other groups. (There's even a fancy name for that natural law principle by which the State nurtures society: *subsidiarity.*) All our wonderful freedoms are rooted, then, in the natural law. *Rights* flow from *nature.* No one has a *right* to do what is *wrong.*

Obviously, then, moral relativism is *not* the most "American" position—quite the opposite. Back to my relativist friend: How can I systematically explain how the natural law actually works?

Imagine yourself discussing a "hot button" issue such as euthanasia or abortion, and the issue of relativism surfaces. Your friend says that you are just spouting your opinion, and that all moral truth is relative. How might you proceed?

1. Recall that at the most foundational level, by the habit technically named *synderesis*, we know that good should be done and pursued and evil should be avoided. So the very fact that you are discussing the issue with someone means that the two of you are aware of what is "good" and "evil." That's the natural law working inside the two of you, in a very basic way.

Now, your conversation partner may *claim* to be a relativist—someone who insists that good and bad is simply a matter of mere opinion. But the relativist actually makes an absolute claim in stating that "everything is relative." Again, if someone ever says that everything is relative, just ask, "Do you insist on that absolutely?" In a word, there is something called "the good" out there, like it or not. This provides us a great starting point (see *VS* 51.2, 59.2, 67.2, and *CCC* 1780).

2. Next, there are a number of very specific examples of what "the good" is, and about which you can probably get your discussion partner to agree. Let's focus on one in particular: It is good to uphold the dignity of the human person.

Many documents of the Magisterium put the point philosophically: *A person should always be treated as an end, not as a means.* In simpler terms, no one should be "used" or turned into a mere object for someone else's utilitarian ends.

We should love people and use things, not use people and love things. *Gaudium et Spes* says, in a text often used by John

Paul II, that the human being is the only creature God willed "for its own sake"—that is, not as an instrumental means to some other good.[8] This truth can be termed the *personalist principle.*

Many today wish to apply relativism to the value of human life, arguing that personhood is not absolutely, but only relatively, applicable to all human beings. But the lines drawn in such application, based on convenience, are highly arbitrary. Those who insist that the complexity of human life demands such arbitrariness should be asked: "So you yourselves, I take it, will not take offense if and when someone else (a murderer or thief, for instance), up against the complexity of his own existence, sees the need to draw some arbitrary lines and treat *you* as a non-person?"

In a word, no one in his or her right mind stands for a relativistic view of human dignity. As Catholic writer Peter Kreeft notes: "The relativist lets the cat out of the bag when you practice what he preaches, when you *act* toward *him* as if his own philosophy of relativism were true. *He* may *preach* relativism, but he expects *you* to *practice* absolutism."[9] Kreeft gives the example of telling his relativist-leaning students that all women in the class will flunk. Given their own relativistic premises, they have no argument to make against such a blatantly unfair practice.

We have thus established a fundamental principle, the personalist principle (or the principle of *subjectivity*), on which to build additional arguments about everything from just wages to slavery to the nature of marriage. We have done this with simple rational argumentation that cuts across divergent religious beliefs. That all humans are persons—this is a truth you "can't not know." A variety of additional basic principles stem from the dignity of the human person: It is good to live peaceably with one another in society, to seek the truth, to nurture our children.[10]

3. The next step is to move to specific moral norms, such as "Don't intentionally kill innocent people" and "Don't commit adultery." Often these norms come across as heteronomous— a big list of things you don't do because God told you not to. But in fact all these norms, as noted in *VS* 13.2 and 52.1, are concrete reflections of the dignity of the human person. When we follow these norms, we are respecting people's dignity, treating them as persons rather than as objects.

The "second table" of the Ten Commandments fits here. It contains moral norms of the natural law, and the Israelites, a stubborn people (like us!), needed a reminder from God himself—a divine Revelation—of what was already written on their hearts, the natural law. The natural virtues—prudence, justice, temperance and fortitude, and the numerous other virtues that organize under these four—help to perfect and fulfill the natural law.[11]

4. Finally, conscience (recall chapter one) is that judgment by which we apply the natural law and the natural virtues to our very particular situations.[12] Often this is a relatively easy application, though following it out can be demanding. (I must be patient with my neighbor; I must not seek revenge.) At other times it takes some "conscientious" scrutiny. (What is the most magnanimous way to confront my neighbor about a problem?)

Great. Now let's say I've convinced my friend that moral truth—the natural law—must exist. Explain how to move from there to a concrete moral issue, such as euthanasia or abortion.

Today, when explaining the natural law to someone, it is best to start with two issues that everyone already agrees upon: slavery and sexism. The reason why everyone agrees that slavery and sexism are wrong is that they so clearly violate the personalist principle as just outlined. They draw arbitrary lines based on race or gender and then treat a whole class of people as objects to be used rather than as persons.

Note that in our two examples we find a biological basis for our natural law claim. That is, in both instances, we recognize that the biological category "human" is operative, and we recognize that all those who bear the biological mark "human" ought to be treated as persons. We might say that the biological category "human" speaks a language: "I am human, I ought to be treated as a person."

Imagine a fireman bravely ascending a ladder. Through the flames and smoke he sees a blur of objects. As he gets closer, he sees that three such objects are in fact human beings—of varied races and genders. Other objects include a violin, a case of photo albums, a fish tank, and the like.

What does he do? He would like to save everything—if time allows. But first he saves the human beings, and without discriminating on the basis of race or gender.

Note two things that have occurred. First, a biological category, "human," was a signal to him of something that was of absolute value. The other objects in the burning room were of relative value. They were instrumental goods, things to be used.

The biological phenomenon "human" sent a signal, contained a profound meaning. The body speaks a language, a philosophical and theological language, and in fact this is precisely what the "theology of the body" is all about. As we'll develop the discussion later, the biological categories "male" and "female" also speak a profound language about marital love and procreation.

Second, note that the fireman didn't need to make a philosophical or theological investigation before figuring out what to do. The natural law, planted right in the body, sent him a signal and he picked it up spontaneously, almost intuitively.[13] If someone asked him why he risked his life to save other human beings, he would think that a strange question—it was just the right thing to do. We have a *natural inclination* within us to respond properly to the natural law.[14]

Any chance the natural law could apply to marriage? I'm involved in a dispute with someone over "homosexual marriage," and we're at a stalemate. My friend says everyone's religious beliefs have to be allowed, and some people believe in different forms of marriage.

I've got just the category for you: "natural marriage." Your friend is right about not forcing a particular *religious* view of marriage on everyone. But we should all agree on some basic standards for marriage, based on our natural inclinations, particularly our natural inclination to treat others as persons, not objects.

Does your friend favor legalizing polygamy? Why not? Because in polygamy, human persons, women especially, tend to be treated as disposable objects, rather than as *nonsubstitutable persons*—which is what a spouse should be. So natural marriage is *permanent* and *exclusive*.

Next, consider the dignity of the children who arrive upon the scene. Don't they deserve, as persons, the stability that comes from a committed couple? Here we only trace the beginnings of an argument for "natural marriage"—see the web site for more.

The natural law argumentation seems airtight. Why doesn't everyone agree with it and follow it?

In one sense you're right: If you master the four steps taken thus far, you will find that no one can defeat your natural law argumentation. To anyone who objects, continue to point out that they are contradicting themselves, because they would never wish to be treated as objects themselves.

In short, they cannot help but agree with the basic principles of the natural law that they "can't not know." They already desire to be treated as persons, not objects. In so desiring, they cannot then deny that right to others.

They already hold that slavery and sexism are wrong. They cannot, then, suddenly claim that other arbitrary lines can be drawn around, say, the unborn or the aged or handicapped. All people are *naturally inclined* toward these truths of the natural law, and all you are doing is articulating that toward which they are naturally inclined.

The difficulties begin to arise as soon as we apply the same set of principles to additional concrete cases, especially cases that are highly controversial, such as abortion, euthanasia, homosexuality, new birth technologies, and contraception (more on all these later). In every instance, some people will disagree with the natural law for one simple reason: It is not always convenient to follow the natural law. Our concupiscent tendency sets to work, and we take the easy and convenient path.

Notice the battle going on within us: On the one hand, we are *naturally inclined* to follow the natural law (recall the example of the fireman). On the other hand, because we have inherited original sin, we have a concupiscent tendency within us—it is part of our fallen nature and it can feel *very natural* to us not to follow the natural law.

We might say that, because of our fallen condition, the natural law *doesn't come naturally*. That's why, even though the natural law is "written on our hearts," many people don't follow it or even acknowledge it.[15] And as we'll see in a bit, that's also one good reason why it is imprudent to legislate the whole of the natural law.

Let's connect the battle just described—between our natural inclinations and concupiscence—to the earlier "battle of the goods" we discovered in chapter one. There, we noted that people tend to seek what they think is good. They generally don't go around trying to do evil—and this corresponds to what we have just labeled our "natural inclinations."

Nevertheless, people do sin, and sin *means* doing evil. This corresponds to the concupiscent tendency just discussed. We solved this problem by showing that when people sin, they are in fact choosing a good, but a good that is disordered, not aligned under the highest good. They are naturally inclined to the good, but concupiscence easily gets in the way of seeking the *properly ordered good* to which they are naturally inclined.

Now that we've covered the natural law, where does human law fit? So many people today say that "you can't legislate morality." I just saw a bumper sticker that said, "Get your laws off my body."

Half of the truth is there. It is true that you can't legislate religious truths. It's true that you can't legislate virtues—imagine laws enforcing gratitude or patience! And it's true that legislation itself should be limited to those matters that clearly affect other people. If that's what it means to "not legislate morality," fine.

But all that doesn't add up to mean that no morality can be legislated. In fact, just the opposite is the case. You can't help but legislate morality; the only question is, Which morality will you legislate?

To clarify this point, imagine the "values clarification" approach to education in some of our public schools. The teacher leads discussions and helps students articulate their feelings and thoughts about hot button moral issues. Students are taught to "own" their own "values" sincerely, and any mention that some values might be better than others is considered intolerant.

Such a method epitomizes the danger of focusing on the good or sincere conscience to the exclusion of the true conscience, as discussed earlier. This method is not neutral at all. It is a thinly disguised relativism, and insofar as it is forced upon students, the pedagogical method is a thinly disguised coercion.

Similarly, the idea that we can't legislate morality is a thin disguise for legalizing relativistic morality. With the force of the State, this form of relativism becomes a "thinly disguised totalitarianism," as John Paul II notes in *CA* 41. To be "neutral" about, say, the absolute dignity of each individual, or the definition of marriage, or the priority of the family, is to take a relativistic stance toward those realities. In *VS* 101 the pope warns against "an alliance between democracy and ethical relativism, which would remove any sure moral reference point from political and social life, and on a deeper level make the acknowledgment of truth impossible."

The best proof that we often legislate morality is the law against slavery. If anyone ever claims "You can't legislate morality," ask if *that* law should be changed, especially for those who would find slaveholding convenient. Make the same point to those sporting the bumper sticker "Get your laws off my body," noting that numerous people are free today precisely because we built laws, based on the natural law, disallowing unjust treatment on the basis of a bodily characteristic—race.

In fact, legislation based on the body is *essential* for treating all humans as persons. Humanness is a biological characteristic, easy to recognize. A just society treats all humans as persons—no exceptions, old or young, in the womb or born, male or female, black, white, or red.

I've got a great solution to getting lots of people ordering their lives under the natural law. Couldn't we base all our civil laws on natural law? In fact, wouldn't the ideal society be one in which the natural law itself constituted civil law?

Sorry—that would spell disaster. While all laws legislate morality, it does not follow that *all* of morality should be legislated. As St. Thomas put it, "Human law cannot punish or forbid all evil deeds: since while aiming at doing away with all evils, it would do away with many good things, and would hinder the advance of the common good" (91, 4).

Thomas goes on to explain that while virtuous people are capable of a very high standard of morality (think of the person for whom it would be virtually unthinkable to drink excessively), other people are not realistically capable of that standard (think of the person who would never drive while drunk, but who at times becomes inebriated in his own home). If human law were to enforce too high a standard (all public *and* private drunkenness is against the law), many citizens would be unduly frustrated and end up without much respect for *any* of the law. Because of this difference in people, human law need not repress all vices but "only the most grievous vices, from which it is possible for the majority to abstain." Further, among grievous vices, the human law should concern itself chiefly with "those that are to the hurt of others" (96, 2).

Thomas, in a word, is most conscious of the phenomenon of concupiscence, also discussed above. Due to it, the natural law written in man's heart often is not followed.

We find here the answer to one of the central secular objections to natural law: If everyone has a natural inclination toward certain goods and truths, then why do people in fact act so differently in this regard? From this point, ethical systems containing various degrees of relativism are built. The reason people act differently is not because truth is relative, or because people are incapable of knowing the truth. Rather, concupiscence draws people away from the truth.[16]

Such an understanding of the limitations of human law might seem somewhat dim and pessimistic. But it is in fact the realistic aspect of a very noble view of human law. Law's nobility lies in its goal: to help make people virtuous.

It is true that law cannot manufacture virtuous habits in people's hearts. But it can lead them to do the *kinds of acts virtuous people do.*[17] (Think here of training wheels on a bicycle.) Then, as people become accustomed to such acts, and find that they are actually happier now that they are acting in accord with their nature, they may gradually develop the actual *habits* that produce such acts. Now, they do the good because they are habituated to it, not because the law forced them to do it.

If everyone were virtuous, we wouldn't need human law at all! But since that is far from the case, law provides a good impetus for people that might lead them to virtue. And since we cannot push people beyond their limits too hastily, we are back to the realism that prevents us from over-legislating morality.

Looks like law can lead people to virtue, but can't force them to be virtuous. Training wheels can lead a child to ride the bike, but can't force him to do it. Do I have it right?

Yes, and this is a good opportunity to explain a bit more what a *virtuous* person is. Usually through arduous practice, individuals can arrive at a point where following the natural law actually does "come naturally." That is what a habit is—something that comes naturally due to practice. It can be a good habit—a virtue—or a bad habit—a vice. (See *CCC* 1803–4.)

Imagine two people, maybe two coaches or two music instructors, both engaging in an act of patience. Though their actions look pretty much identical, one has struggled enormously to produce a few acts of patience, while the other has developed the actual good habit, or virtue, of patience, out of which her patient acts naturally flow. Which of the two do you admire more?

Many of us are quick to point to the one who struggles—after all, that one has succeeded in doing the right thing after intense struggle, while the other had it pretty easy. But it's the truly virtuous person we should admire most (and if we admire people struggling, we can be assured that even the habitually patient person struggled to become patient, and still struggles a good deal with some other areas of life). Our goal as moral agents is not just to do the kind of acts virtuous people do, but to become truly virtuous people.

It is the full life of virtue that the rich young man (*VS* 6) shied away from. Virtue is where the real action is in the moral life, and the arena where real growth in holiness occurs. *VS* 52 notes that there is no upper limit here, and this is what allows for the incredible diversity and uniqueness of each person striving to live the Catholic moral life.

We all should share a common foundation, avoiding all the evils that Christ, through the Church, prohibits. Above that, the sky is the limit. This is the open-ended life of virtue where uniqueness truly flourishes. No one practices the virtues in exactly the same way. We each bring our uniqueness to them.

> The fact that only the negative commandments oblige always and under all circumstances does not mean that in the moral life prohibitions are more important than the obligation to do good indicated by the positive commandments. The reason is this: The commandment of love of God and love of neighbor does not have in its dynamic any higher limit, but it does have a lower limit, beneath which the commandment is broken. (*VS* 52)

That is, there is no upper limit to the life of virtue, but the moral bedrock provides a lower limit under which we must not fall if we are to stay in right relation to God, neighbor, and self.

Some examples: The virtue of purity requires a great deal of effort and prayer. While we can be expected not to break the absolute norms regarding sexuality, the development of a pure mind is an ongoing project in virtue.

Likewise, acting charitably is a lifelong project that cannot be summed up in a few absolute norms. There are many actions contrary to charity that are forbidden, summed up in what might be called the "silver rule": *Don't* do unto others as you would *not* have them do unto you.[18] But the full life of charity is a unique, personal lifelong journey summed up in the "golden rule": *Do* unto others what you would have them *do* unto you.

Imagine building your dream house. The builder can give

you absolute answers about your foundation and about its absolute importance. Foundations aren't unique or aesthetically pleasing. But the house itself, that one-of-a-kind log chalet in the mountains, is unique beyond measure.

The architect and builder cannot tell you exactly how to design it. They can point you in many right directions. But the plan for your dream home is yours. Likewise with the relationship between absolute moral norms and the full life of virtue. We'll return to the topic of the virtues in chapter eight—an appropriate way to conclude our journey.

That's a nice analogy, and I'll borrow it for my next question. It seems as if not a few theologians and pastors have not only been building rather disastrous houses over the past few decades, but also have all but forgotten how to build a solid foundation. Does *VS* address this problem?

I borrowed the analogy from a friend.[19] Amid its positive and creative promulgation of participated theonomy, at regular intervals *VS* firmly warns against the erroneous moral theories that have arisen (4.2; 29.4). These theories include: a false understanding of freedom (the warning is in *VS* 34.2; 37.2), a reductionist view of conscience and natural law (54.2; 56), a faulty understanding of the body/person relationship (48.3), a sloppy understanding of sin (67), an incomplete grasp of the "moral object" (75; 76.2), an unfaithful stance toward the Magisterium (113.2), and a failure to integrate Christ and his grace into the moral life (37.2).

This book treats each of these problems. Each erroneous

theory is an instance of what we can call "revisionist" moral theology—the term actually used by theologians positing these theories.

Remarkably, while being firm as can be, the pope refrains from letting the encyclical turn into a heteronomous diatribe against such errors. He seizes the high ground and takes the opportunity to advance a positive proclamation of the good life. Listen to what he says in 83.2:

> Dear Brothers in the Episcopate, we must not be content merely to warn the faithful about the errors and dangers of certain ethical theories. We must first of all show the inviting splendor of that truth which is Jesus Christ himself. In him who is the Truth (see Jn 14:6), man can understand fully and live perfectly, through his good actions, his vocation to freedom in obedience to the divine law summarized in the commandment of love of God and neighbor. And this is what takes place through the gift of the Holy Spirit, the Spirit of truth, of freedom and of love: in him we are enabled to interiorize the law, to receive it and to live it as the motivating force of true personal freedom: "the perfect law, the law of liberty" (Jas 1:25).

Each theme of participated theonomy is present in that fine summation of what VS sets out to accomplish. We can imitate the pope's splendid example by always placing our firm defense of the Church's moral doctrine in a positive, friendly and non-polemical context.

FOUR

THE NATURAL LANGUAGE OF THE BODY

I know that the word "nature" in natural law does not refer to trees and birds, but to the nature given to us by the Creator. Just as there are physical laws for physical nature, there are moral laws for our human nature. Still, when I think of the "natural law," I wonder: Does it include some aspect of our own human biological nature?

Try this multiple-choice test:

1. Would you prefer to say (a) "I am a soul occupying a body" or (b) "I am a person, with both a soul and a body"?
2. Would you prefer to say (a) "I am a person who *happens* to be female (or male)," or (b) "I am a female (or male) person."

I'm sure you aced the quiz; it should be "b" for both answers. And you're in good company: John Paul II notes in *VS* that "it is in the unity of body and soul that the person is the subject of his own moral acts" (48). Of course we *distinguish* the spiritual/rational part of our nature from the physical part of our nature, but when we do, we are distinguishing two elements of *the one person.*

People who too quickly separate the two fall into the error called *dualism.* They would think of the body as "raw material" on which to act: "I'll do what I want with my body." Sometimes they treat the body well (jogging, taking vitamins, eating healthily). But sometimes they don't (abortion, contraception, new birth technologies, euthanasia, cloning, masturbation, premarital sex, adultery).

They don't want someone else telling them what to do (heteronomy). So they decide to be their own arbiters (autonomy). But if they make themselves arbiters over the body, what are they missing out on?

You guessed it—participated theonomy. God's truth is actually revealed in and through the dynamism of the body. Earlier we discussed how we are "naturally inclined" to follow the natural law. Our "natural inclinations" include both a bodily element and also a spiritual and rational element that distinguishes us from the animals.

Think of the body "speaking" to you in what John Paul II and others term the "language of the body." Our biological dynamisms don't speak verbally, of course, and so they don't give us—on their own—complete answers to moral questions. But they provide an excellent *starting point* for figuring out the right way to treat the body. "The person ... discovers in the body the anticipatory signs, the expression and the promise of the gift of self, in conformity with the wise plan of the Creator" (*VS* 48). Thus the body "speaks a language," a language of anticipatory signs, providing parameters within which we live the moral life.

What a beautiful understanding of the body! How could anyone even consider an "autonomous" view that treats the body as mere raw material? Let me guess—they're reacting to a heteronomous understanding of the body. Am I right? Can you explain this?

You're really getting the hang of what the pope is doing in *VS!* An error—a heteronomous one—was made in some forms of natural law theory. The mistake was to locate moral truth directly in the physical dimension alone, yielding a kind of "physicalism": Here are the natural ends of bodily organs, now follow them.

Given this approach, it is easy to imagine that Catholic teaching asks us to be like animals, following our biology, minimizing or eliminating our uniqueness as persons. Not surprisingly, then, someone once called Catholic teaching on sexual matters a "barnyard morality."

But wait a minute! If the traditional natural law emphasis really succumbed to a brute physicalism that reduced humans to the animal level, then why did it not allow human beings simply to follow their "instinctive" passions? Let's play a little game to illustrate the situation.

Pretend that you really do belong to a church that uses a purely physicalistic natural law theory. What would the moral norms of such a church look like? Try these "Ten Commandments":

I.   Mate with anyone as you like. (Polygamy welcome.)

II.   Defend your own bodily integrity at all costs. (No firemen and policemen, please.)

III.   Never give your life for another or for the faith. (No martyrs around here.)

IV.   No technological changes are to be made to the body. (Cancel that hip replacement surgery.)

V.   Have as many children as physically possible. (Ignore physical, psychological, and financial hardship).

VI.   No celibacy permitted. (You'd be repressing your instincts.)

VII.   Survival of the fittest rules. (Let the weak die out; they don't matter anyway.)

VIII.   Eat, eat, and eat.

IX.   Drink, drink, and drink.

X.   Capstone commandment: Indulge yourself.

Does that sound like your Church? It may be true that at times the traditional natural law position was articulated poorly, with primary reference to following biological laws, and little emphasis on the person. Today, when we look back at that approach, it certainly looks heteronomous. But by no means was the *content* itself of the natural law, as taught by the Church, merely a matter of biology. The genuine natural law tradition embraced by Catholicism places the physical dimension within the broader context of human personhood.[1]

Today we're better able to articulate the personalist dimensions of the natural law—which is precisely the approach of participated theonomy. The body provides "rational indicators," "reference points," or "anticipatory signs" (*VS* 48). Then the *person*—you and I—set out to listen to that language of the body.

We have some rather impressive equipment to bring to the task: our intellects, divine revelation, and free will. We all have the responsibility to grasp or "mine" the meaning of the body, and then to align ourselves freely with the meaning. The meaning is then really ours.

The transcendent truth that the Creator has infused into the body is not a heteronomous imposition. Rather, it's something that each person participates in: The truth is carried in each person's own body, and each person freely grasps and lives that truth, making it his or her own.

We've just shown how the inadequate heteronomous understanding of the body needed to be "fixed" with participated theonomy. But guess how numerous revisionist theologians reacted instead? You can fill in the blank: autonomy.

They accused the Church of biologism. That is, they claimed that the Catholic moral tradition forces us to be slaves to the body, rather than exerting our personal freedom over and against the raw material of the body. In reaction, these theologians went on to dissociate God's plan from our biology (*VS* 47). They separated body and person, claiming that each person must determine the meaning of the body for him or herself.

Remember what that split is called? It is a *dualism* of person and body. Catholic doctrine overcomes that dualism by showing the close connection between person and body. The body contains a meaning planted in it by the Creator, a transcendent meaning.

Read *VS*: 47–53.

It's fascinating to consider that the body actually speaks a language that helps us inform our moral lives. What does it say? What is the content of the language?

Let's retrieve something we said earlier regarding human dignity, this time emphasizing the role biology plays. Anyone possessing a human nature ought to be respected as a person with a right to life. "Human nature" is a biological category—a biologist can tell us that an unborn baby, an elderly person with a debilitating disease, people of other races, are human.

This humanity speaks a language: "I am human, I ought to be treated as a person." It is wrong arbitrarily to treat some humans as persons and some not. This arbitrary discrimination is what links the issues of abortion, slavery, and genocide.

Too often people claim that pro-life views entail forcing a religious view on everyone. But in fact the sanctity of all human life is easily determined without reference to religious arguments, first by establishing that the being in question is human, and second by noting that all humans should be treated as persons. The "language" spoken by the biological category "human" is the basis of the dignity of the human person, and this dignity is the foundation stone of every aspect of Catholic morality, from sexual ethics to social ethics. Remember, that's part of what makes moral norms more than just heteronomous rules.

At some time or other, nature's "clock" runs down and we die. Until that time, there is a thread—however slender at times—of health, of life, in us. We ought never interfere with that thread of health. It speaks a language to us: We ought never decide to end life at a time we determine on our own, regardless of how good our intentions might be in so doing.

God is the arbiter of life and death, and through biological nature he alone appoints the time of death. To interfere is to misuse our intellect and will, playing God rather than assenting to his will, manifested in the language of the body. We may, of course, use our intellects in the discovery and the application of scientific and medical means for enhancing or healing the body, though even such technology can be misused in situations where life is "forced" on a terminally ill person with disproportionate treatment.

Now it should be easy to understand why it's permissible (if tragic at times) to euthanize an animal, but not permissible to euthanize humans. Animals, wonderful as many of them are, do not have the same personal meaning built into their bodily dynamisms. That is why we "use" animals—though we must be careful to use, not abuse, them. We are to be stewards over creation, using it responsibly.

The human body has a *personal* language. To ignore it, and to treat humans as animals, is to treat ourselves and others as objects. Earlier we mentioned the philosophical language John Paul II likes to use: We should never treat others as means to an end, but rather as persons who are ends in themselves. Now let's take an important additional step.

When someone treats you well, as a person, you *appreciate* it, as you appreciate a *gift*. "The person, by the light of reason and the support of virtue, discovers in the body the anticipatory signs, the expression and the promise of the gift of self, in conformity with the wise plan of the Creator. It is in the light of the dignity of the human person—a dignity which must be affirmed for its own sake—that reason grasps the specific moral value of certain goods towards which the person is naturally inclined" (*VS* 50).

When we treat one another as persons, we are treating one another as *gifts* rather than as objects. So we might say that the language the body speaks is the language of self-gift. When we listen to that language and follow it, the gift of self is made in, through, and by means of actions that respect the transcendent meaning of the body.

I love that phrase, the "transcendent meaning" of the body, because it affords the body so much dignity. Too often in our culture the body is cheapened. How closely is this transcendent meaning tied to the Catholic faith? Do you have to be Catholic to appreciate this profound meaning of the body?

If you were to tell a friend, "It sure was unfair that you got used," she would understand immediately and would not perceive any imposition of religious dogma. The meaning of the body is part of the natural law, which we know intuitively, and can understand with our intellects.

But God's revelation adds immeasurably to that natural knowledge. The language of self-gift that inheres in the body is none other than the Trinitarian language of the God in whose image we are made—and the *natural* knowledge we possess is but a rational participation, slender but important, in that *revealed* Trinitarian knowledge. As noted in *GS* 24:

> The Lord Jesus, when he prayed to the Father "that all may be one ... as we are one" (Jn 17:21-22), opened up vistas closed to human reason. For he implied a *certain likeness* between the union of the divine Persons and the union of God's children in truth and charity. This likeness reveals that man, who is the only creature on earth which God willed for its own sake, cannot fully find himself except through a sincere gift of self.

Put another way, a person can have the full substance of personhood only by nurturing the relational side of personhood. To be a person, to find oneself and be true to oneself, is to be relational, to give the gift of self.[2]

Unconditional self-giving is precisely what happens in the relations between the Father, the Son, and the Holy Spirit. We are made in the image of the Trinity, and so we receive "the call to give oneself in love to another person, and to receive in turn his or her gift of self."[3] "The human body, with its sex, and its masculinity and femininity ... includes right from the beginning the nuptial attribute, that is, the capacity of expressing love, that love in which the person becomes a gift and—by means of this gift—fulfills the meaning of his being and existence."[4]

John Paul II gives a name to this language of self-giving that is infused into the body: the *nuptial meaning* of the body. He goes so far as to claim that "the awareness of the meaning of the body ... in particular its nuptial meaning—is the fundamental element of existence in the world."[5]

So far so good: The body speaks a language, and that language is one of self-gift. Now, how does this apply to concrete issues of morality?

A host of concrete issues are illumined when we examine how God uses the human body to create new life. Try to imagine God creating new human lives on his own. He would will a new baby, find a willing couple, and *zap*, there the child would be!

Instead, however, he works in, through, and by means of married couples. God has given them, through nature, a set of instruments to use on their special mission to help him in the creation (procreation) of children. As noted in *EV* 42, a "certain sharing by man in God's lordship is also evident in the *specific responsibility* which he is given *for human life as such*. It is a responsibility which reaches its highest point in the giving of life *through procreation* by man and woman in marriage."

What are these special gifts, these instruments given to couples for their "special assignment"? Fertility and sexual intercourse. When female fertility (the male being always fertile) and sex intersect, *that's precisely where God will create a baby if he wants to do so.*

Would you refer to these instruments as "merely biological"?

They are certainly biological, but they are a lot more besides—the biology is infused with a profound meaning. They are the unique instruments that couples use to participate in God's plan for them to procreate.

Note the powerful sense of participated theonomy here. On the one hand, we do not autonomously determine the meaning of these instruments—we are to respect these instruments, respecting the "language" they speak.[6] On the other hand, God does not just use couples apart from their free and dignified participation. God's ordered way of doing things is planted right in the bodies of the couple, and the couple is to listen to and respond to the language of the body—a true partaking in God's plan.

Let's "focus in" on the equipment that God has given the couple, through which he can create new life if he so wills. The conjugal act during the fertile part of the cycle is the most important part of that equipment. Call it the "sacred interplay of fertility and sexual intercourse," or "sacred interplay" for short.

If God wills to create new life, that is the "space" where he can get busy. Remember, God will infuse the *immaterial* aspect of the new person, the soul, into the *material* aspect that he creates through the couple. We should think of this not as two separate events, but a single event in which we can distinguish the action of God and the action of the couple.

In this way God ties his creativity to the cooperative work of the couple. So how should the couple treat this sacred space within which God can create new life? Only with the highest respect.

An essential component of the spouses' self-gift to each other is, with that other, a profound respect for the sacred interplay. Destroying that interplay also damages the mutual gift of self. Among the various reasons the couple marry should be the commitment to tread that sacred interplay together, and to tread it respectfully. That commitment is a great mutual gift, one to the other. Not to respect the sacred interplay is to *withhold* a substantial portion of that mutual gift of self.

Their mutual self-gift holds within itself that great gift of the sacred interplay provided by God. By reverencing this gift, they in turn give a great gift back to God. They say to God, "We are willing to cooperate with you; we give ourselves over to you." Their marriage is a *participation* in God's providential *order*.

Sounds like participated theonomy to me! But then, aren't couples withholding the gift of self and *not* cooperating with

God when they intentionally *avoid* intercourse during fertile times? And isn't that the same as contraception?

Couples can respect and participate in the sacred interplay in two ways: by making use of it—using the conjugal act during the fertile time—and by keeping a certain distance from it—abstaining during the fertile time. An analogy may be helpful, and I hope you enjoy mountains because they play a central role in the analogy.

Imagine yourself headed toward your favorite national forest with a fine mountain in order to get some fresh air and do some hiking. A sense of awe overwhelms you as the mountains gradually come into sight. When you actually arrive at the base of the mountains, you will either climb or not climb, depending on numerous contingencies—weather, how you feel, trail conditions, and the like.

You use the virtue of prudence to decide. If prudence dictates that you climb, you set off, but with due caution and with a profound sense of awe. If prudence dictates that you not climb, you are still filled with a genuine awe at the power the mountain holds, and you spend your time hiking the numerous other splendid paths that this special region holds for you. To get to the peak, you'll have to wait a few days, or come another time.

Whether or not you climb to the peak, you will have shown respect for this special, sacred space. Likewise with the instruments of fertility. The couple might enter that sacred space, using the conjugal act during the fertile time. Or they might in good conscience have realized that now is not a prudent time to have a child, and so they abstain from that sacred space.

Either way, there is a reverence for it as God's special territory. If he is to create a child, it will be in and through the sacred interplay of sex and fertility.

Note well that the conjugal act during an infertile time is itself highly sacred, but sacred in a way distinct from what we have termed the sacred interplay of sex and fertility. To borrow from the analogy, the entire region is very special. But there is something distinctly special about the glorious mountain that graces the region.

Both spouses show reverence for the sacred interplay *together*. God has built their bodies in such a way that they, in giving themselves to each other in marriage, participate in his creation of the gift of life, and the spouses ought to respect that profound meaning that inheres in their bodies. Again, their marital gift of themselves to each other includes openness to the gift of life that God can give through that very marital gift.

Compare this gift-giving with what animals do: The couple's biology has a *personal* meaning that an animal's biology does not have. (They have the biological part but not the personal part.) To show disrespect for that meaning would be to treat each other as animals instead of as persons. We spay and neuter animals because their biology does not carry a transcendent meaning. As stewards over creation, we treat them with respect—for instance, we should avoid all cruelty to animals—but not the respect due to *persons*.

Unfortunately it is all too easy, and convenient, for us to take total control over this sacred ground, arbitrating over it as if it were "all ours," reducing it to the level of objects. Again our analogy can serve us: It is possible to wreck a mountain. We can actually turn a beautiful mountain into a *different kind of place*.

Think of devastating deforestation or reckless use of fire. Don't you agree that certain mountains ought to be largely left as they are? Of course, we can use technology to make improvements that respect the basic nature of the mountain—for instance, we can blaze a trail and do all sorts of things that protect against erosion. But these improvements do not change the nature of the mountain. Technology is wonderful, inasmuch as it works within and not outside the parameters of things sacred.

I see exactly where this is going: The "theology of the body" reveals exactly the problem with contraception. Using the analogy, is contraception like wrecking the mountain? And is natural family planning actually a matter of respecting God's creative space?

You've got it. Just as it is possible to destroy the environment, it is possible to arbitrate over the "sacred interplay," turning it into something of a very different kind. It is possible—and convenient—to treat this sacred interplay in a way that refuses God the opportunity to make use of his special place. Then the couple place God outside of the marriage, which then becomes the couple's own territory over which they alone arbitrate.

That's what contraception and sterilization do. Couples who have gone through some or much of their marriages without a correct sense of this sacred ground, and the sacred interplay to which they have been entrusted, may sense the deepest regret for having damaged it, at least in part. It is at the point of this realization that couples must remember Christ's all-encompassing forgiveness for all sin.

In our age many Catholic couples may have been invincibly ignorant. Many were taught virtually the opposite of Catholic doctrine: "Here's the official teaching, but the Church also tells us to follow our consciences, so ..." Those taught the doctrine often caught a heteronomous rendition of it: "It's true because the pope said so"—correct, but hardly sufficient. In sum, the truth about this great mystery must always be accompanied by the truth about forgiveness.

And now on to natural family planning (NFP). God wants the couple to cooperate with him. He has given them the sacred interplay, and he has also given them another space— the infertile times—during which sexual intercourse will not intersect with fertility. This cooperation—think "participated theonomy"—involves the couple's own conscientious decisions about family size.

It is expected that couples will, to a greater or lesser extent, avoid the conjugal act during the fertile period. When they do so, in good conscience, they are respecting the profound meaning contained in the fertility cycle. They never deny the sacred interplay; rather they affirm it, either in trying to conceive or in deciding that conception would be imprudent in certain circumstances. They avoid treating the conjugal act as a different kind of act, an act that denies this sacred interplay—namely, a contraceptive act.[7]

In using natural family planning, the couple is like the people in our analogy who are headed toward the mountain, watching for it to appear in all its grandeur. They are watching for the "sacred space" to appear, aware that this will be a time either to "engage" the sacred interplay or not to so engage. They are not watching for the "danger zone" or the "unsafe time," though that is unfortunately a common terminology used by some well-intentioned teachers of NFP. Rather they are watching for a unique time of sacred mystery.

Again, keep in mind that the *entire* arena of conjugal love is infused with transcendent meaning. Think of it this way: The broad meaning of the whole marital relationship is the larger context within which the more specific procreative meaning exists.

Does the idea of the "sacred interplay" also help us in our thinking about the "new birth technologies" such as *in vitro* fertilization, and maybe even cloning?

Let's start with couples struggling with infertility. So often they feel entirely cut off from the procreative meaning of conjugal love. But in fact they give witness to that meaning in a profound, though most painful, way.

Infertile couples often have far more respect and awe for the "sacred interplay" than anyone else. They *engage* that interplay, all the while knowing that, barring a miracle, it will not yield a child. (Eventually, this happens to all couples after menopause.) Also consider those with the homosexual inclination who courageously are living chastely. They are not to engage the sacred interplay at all.

Right inside the painfulness of these people lies something profoundly positive: a sense of deep homage to the sacredness of the space where God creates new life. We could say that the sense of sacredness is directly proportionate to the pain experienced. The body speaks a language, and in a fallen world it is often a language spoken right in the midst of painful tragedy. God asks us to respect this language, and it is precisely that deep respect that lies behind the *prohibitions* regarding new birth technologies and homosexual acts. Seeing reality through the lens of participated theonomy, we can place those prohibitions within a positive context, a context of respect for a great good.

When thinking about the new birth technologies, I had always thought that the Church didn't like the *technological* aspect. Don't a lot of people think that the Church is "antitechnology"?

That wrong impression comes from a heteronomous understanding of the Church's moral norms. The Church *loves* technology—so long as it doesn't destroy the *meaning* of the body (see *VS* 50: the Church rejects those "manipulations of corporeity" that "alter its human meaning"). For instance, "natural" family planning doesn't mean "natural" as opposed to "artificial." In fact, there are all sorts of technologies available for helping women to chart their cycles accurately.

Rather, "natural" family planning means family planning in accord with the *nature* of the body-person, or more precisely, with the natural truth about the sacred interplay between fertility and sex. Likewise for "natural" procreation juxtaposed with new birth technologies.

Consider for a moment the amazing advances in ultrasound

technology, which allow ever more clear views of the child growing in a mother's womb. (One new machine even allows the mother virtually to touch the child!) Looking at what is clearly a living human being, a mother and father can "hear" the language of the body: "I am a person."

Various new birth technologies, on the other hand, *circumvent* the sacred *means* through which God creates new life. These technologies might produce a good *end,* but they subvert the *mutual self-giving* that is part of the sacred interplay. An essential part of the couple's "giving of self" to the other is a surrender, if you will, to *what God wills* in the context of the sacred interplay. It is here that God will create the gift of a child if he so wills.

Respect for the sacred interplay *is an essential part of the spouses' self-gift to each other*—a willingness to receive this gift, if it is to be given. *The child is a gift, not a right.* With the new birth technologies, the gift becomes something the couple arbitrates over, and so is no longer treated as a gift.

The gift is turned into someone (a baby) to whom the couple has a right. The child is treated as a commodity to which one has a right, instead of a gift granted in the context of the spouses' self-gift. Cloning especially epitomizes the denial of self-gift because it completely severs the child from any cooperation between a man and a woman. And finally, abortion is a logical tragic outflow of the refusal to see the child as a gift.

It is clear from these examples that biology is not just raw data for us to arbitrate over as we please. Biology is a carrier of great transcendent meaning. Once we grasp this point, we are on the right track in understanding numerous issues in the field of "bioethics."

In fact, with this insight we know more than many professional bioethicists, who tend to focus almost exclusively on the notion of "patient autonomy." They are often reacting against a heteronomous view that, in a backwards way, is "antitechnological." As we have seen, however, practices ranging from contraception to cloning are not wrong because of their artificiality. They are wrong in so far as the artificiality interferes with and subverts the language of the body—whether it's the transcendent meaning of the "sacred interplay" or the transcendent and personal meaning of humanness.

Remember, too, that respect for the transcendent meaning of the body is an essential part of what it means to *give the self to others*. Destroying that meaning also damages the mutual gift of self.

Don't you think this material is quite important for couples preparing for marriage? They need to know how easy it is to do all sorts of things, with good intentions perhaps, that prevent genuine self-giving from taking place.

We easily deceive ourselves! It's similar to the "battle of the goods" (chapter one)—for there are all sorts of goods that couples can pursue together in ways that are *not properly ordered*. When properly ordered, a couple is on what we might call the path or "trajectory" of self-giving in their marriage. Then, their marriage is properly aligned with their *ultimate* destiny.

Unfortunately, given our concupiscence, it is immensely easy to pursue marriage in such a way that each spouse "recoils back" upon the self. We often think of this recoiling happening outside of marriage, as indeed it does, but it also happens easily right within a marriage. Then, we are not giving but taking—then we have a "mutual accommodation of two independent egos,"[8] or "mere simultaneous taking" rather than true mutual giving.[9]

It's especially easy to treat sex this way, because it involves partial goods such as pleasure and togetherness, which can easily deceive us into thinking we are pursuing something truly good. That explains why many claim that contraception enhances the marriage, or certain new birth technologies work "just great," or premarital sex is a sharing of love. Such couples are stealing these other goods from their proper place within a much larger context. They are using the body to speak some of the body's truth, but not all of it—they are "lying" with the body,[10] not respecting the true language the body speaks.

Let's focus again on the sacred interplay. When a couple respects this special place (of God's), they are aware that their marital adventure is a mutual self-gift (something *unitive*) that spills over into something beyond themselves (an outflowing of the unity). They give to each other in a way that opens outward to another (a third), and *they do this insofar as they tread on, or around, the ultimate sacred interplay respectfully.*

Pope Paul VI's encyclical *Humanae Vitae* (1968) speaks of the two people's giving as the *unitive* meaning of sexuality, and the opening outward to another as the *procreative* meaning of sexuality. These meanings link up to the Trinitarian view of the person noted earlier: The Son graciously receives the Father's self-gift, and the Father graciously receives back the Son's own self-gift.

And the Holy Spirit? This profound mutual gratitude "explodes" beyond itself, as the love of the Father and Son breathes or "spirates" the Holy Spirit. So married couples *participate* in this Trinitarian *order* of giving. For the mutual giving expands beyond itself in a giving or procreative way.

Now we have an expanded meaning of "procreativity." Although the procreative meaning of marital love is connected with the having of a child, it is not identical with the having of a child, or even necessarily with the intention of having a child. Rather, we can assign the word "procreativity" to the Trinitarian phenomenon of uniting in such a way that there is "an opening outward beyond the two." *Essential to this opening outward is the deep respect for the sacred interplay.*

Now get ready for an amazing idea that can be of immense help to infertile couples. We can distinguish "procreative kinds of acts" from "child-creating kinds of acts," or, if you will, "baby-creating kinds of acts." Many procreative kinds of acts will not be baby kinds of acts—the couple might not have a baby, yet is genuinely opening outward beyond themselves, and this opening outward we name "procreativity."

For that reason, we need not say to infertile couples, "Sorry you can't have the procreative meaning of marital love, but at least you have the unitive meaning." Rather, infertile couples have *both meanings.* The fact that the procreative meaning will not manifest itself in a baby might often be tragic, but it does not detract from the full integrity of marital love.

Before we move on to the next chapter, a quick word to connect the theology of the body to our discussion of natural law: Every point made here is defensible on the basis of the natural law, and the Creator God who is the author of the

natural law. Truths of the divine law greatly enhance these natural truths—and you'll notice above that I slid the Trinity in.

We turn next to a full treatment of the divine law. Think of
it as placing natural truths inside a much broader context that
encompasses, without extinguishing, those natural truths (see
VS 45.2).

I liked what you said earlier—that "following the natural law doesn't come naturally," due to concupiscence. What is the remedy? Isn't the grace of Christ necessary?

Remember the four types of law? Eternal, divine, natural, and human—and now we focus on the divine law, which is another term for divine revelation. Recall from our discussion of participated theonomy that Revelation is not first and foremost a set of data, a list of commandments, but a Person, the person of Christ, mediated to us in and through Scripture and Tradition (see *VS* 88.4). Through him, our Redeemer, we participate in the divine life of the triune God, a participation that places us in right relation with God (justification) and sanctifies our very being.[1] (Read *CCC* 1987–2016.)

We quickly run into a difficulty: How and where do we find Christ? Of course we find him in our hearts, but we have to be able to distinguish the voice of Christ in our hearts from the voice of our own selves. Otherwise the person of Jesus Christ becomes a pliable entity that we can mold according to our own desires, gradually turning him into nothing but a mirror image of the self.

Not surprisingly, God has providentially given us some clear criteria by which we can discern what is the true voice of Christ and what is not. Christ is concretely available to us through the "twin sources" of Revelation, Tradition and Scripture. (Lots more coming on these twin sources, and on the Magisterium that interprets them.)

The divine law is more than a nice "add on" to the natural law. It is more than something that helps us follow the natural law more easily. Think of the divine law—following Christ—as the very heart of Christian ethics, and as encompassing (without extinguishing) the natural law.

To live the good life is to follow Christ. The Christian way of living the good life is not one method alongside other methods, such as the secular way, the Buddhist way, or the Islamic way. Rather, the Christian way is the only way to live the good life.

Does that sound arrogant? Only at first glimpse. Although the only real ethics is Christian ethics, non-Christians *partake in it* in different ways and in different degrees, often unbeknownst to themselves.

Revelation guides and confirms the use of reason, and adds truths that could not be known, or could not be known for sure, by reason alone.[2] The Trinity, the Incarnation, and the sacraments are examples of such truths of faith. The knowledge that our final destiny is eternal union with God, and that God providentially cares for us, are truths of divine revelation.

Now watch this fascinating next point. Once we accept such revealed truths, a very *reasonable* picture of reality emerges. The notion of our final beatific end makes so much sense that it's natural to react with the question "Why didn't *I* think of that?"

Why not? Because it is too majestic! God revealed it, but precisely because it is such a reasonable picture of reality, we immediately think it is the most obvious thing in the world. So, while revealed truths are *beyond* reason, they are *compatible* with reason. That's essential to participated theonomy: God's pattern is friendly to who we are.

We have stressed how the mysteries of the faith need to be integrated into moral theology, for in the past several centuries there was a tendency to treat moral theology in such a way that it seemed removed from the faith. This tendency manifested itself in the "manuals" of moral theology (discussed earlier) written for seminary education, in which Christ, grace, and our final destiny were rarely mentioned.

Without these truths of divine revelation, we end up with—remember that word—a *heteronomous* view of the good life as only a cold set of rules to follow. In reaction, revisionist theologians came up with an *autonomous* way to separate morality from the mysteries of the faith. In this approach, faith is viewed as a general attitude of sincerity and love of God, practiced in community, with the nitty-gritty *content* of the moral life left up to each individual's conscience (see *VS* 37 and 88).

Such an autonomous perspective often appears right within the liturgy. In a noble effort to avoid heteronomy, the Mass is reduced to a community-building exercise. Participated theonomy, on the other hand, grasps the full *content* of the moral life—no vague platitudes here—and integrates it right within a dynamically solid *content*-filled faith in Christ and the Church.

Pardon me, but the Church appears to be speaking out of two sides of her mouth. How can there be a big focus on reason and the natural law, and then a big emphasis on the importance of Revelation, Christ, and grace?

Imagine yourself talking to your roommate (if you're a student) or your colleague (if you're out in the workforce). Let's say she has a bitter taste in her mouth when it comes to things religious. (There was probably a heteronomous version of religion in her upbringing). But an autonomous lifestyle has left her dissatisfied, and she is anxious to speak with someone—yourself, of course—who "has it together."

You can't use your best participated theonomy cards—Christ, heaven, prayer, the call to holiness. She might be ready for that a few years down the road. So instead you pull out all of your "natural law equipment." You show her how she already believes in the natural law, in so far as she holds strongly to the dignity of every person. You gradually move from issues such as slavery and genocide to issues such as abortion and euthanasia. You might even get into the natural portion of the theology of the body!

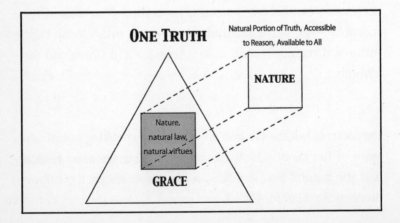

You are using a *portion* of the whole truth, which is Christ. You are seizing upon the portion (or "slice") of the truth, of the eternal law, that the intellect is capable of grasping and the will is capable of affirming. You know perfectly well that you are giving Christ to her, but not explicitly, and not completely.

You know well that the portion of the truth you are using belongs within the compass of the eternal and divine law. But she need not know that right away. This may be her first exposure to the truth presented in a non-heteronomous way. (The very word "truth" sends heteronomous shivers up her spine!)

Participated theonomy is powerful and can be taken in small doses. You provide a small dose, a natural one. It is exciting to know that Christ is at work in her, unknown to herself, as she encounters the natural law.

Consider four *VS* texts that place nature within the compass of grace: 23.2; 73.1; 88.4;103.3.
Read *CCC:* 1965–74.

Can we turn to a related case—the person of another religion, even an atheist, who seems to be highly virtuous? Lots of people proudly claim "you don't have to be Christian to be virtuous," and they quickly add, "Some of the most virtuous people I know are atheists." What would you say about all this?

For purposes of our discussion, let's assume that a particular person's rejection of Christianity or even of God is due to invincible ignorance, and that he is therefore not in a state of mortal sin. The individual is not cooperating with God's grace—if he were, imagine the heights of virtue he might display! But God's grace is operating in him nonetheless, though it is greatly hindered by his lack of awareness of it, and lack of cooperation with it.

Here we get to the most important point about the virtuous atheist. He obviously possesses a great treasure: He has many virtues, and these are due to God's grace acting in him, unknown to him.

The tragedy is that he thinks *he himself*, or perhaps another human such as a parent, is the source of his virtue. The problem with the atheist is often pride, not necessarily that he is a really bad person. He does not know that he'd be nothing without God.

Consider St. Augustine. He was brilliant, with plenty of intellectual virtue, and although he had some rather fierce vices, he must have had numerous moral virtues. He was an excellent teacher who was very effective with his students, and he must have had profound leadership abilities. All of that is not possible without quite an array of virtues.

Augustine's problem was that he refused to recognize the source of those virtues. In his famous autobiography, the *Confessions*, he tells the story of how he gradually and begrudgingly ("Lord, make me chaste, but not yet") came to realize the source of truth, goodness, and beauty. When he finally acknowledges ("confesses") this source, he is aghast at having not recognized it before: "O beauty ever ancient and ever new, late have I loved you. You were within me, and I was in the world, outside myself."

God was in his heart, and he had abandoned his very self where God dwelt. When he finally became aware of God's grace, accepted it, and began to cooperate with it, it was like a floodgate opening up, a vast new potential for developing a serious relationship with the source of everything, and for the flourishing of the spiritual life and the life of virtue.

Let's consider a couple of key texts. *LG* 14–16 contains a profound reflection on the relationship between the Catholic Church (the one true Church) and those who are in *partial communion* with it through baptism, those members of other religions who are *related* to it, and even those who through invincible ignorance are likewise related to it. A critical phrase in article 16 says that those who are *related* to the Church are so related "not without grace." Likewise, *GS* 22 speaks of the "hidden grace" operative in those who are outside the Church, through invincible ignorance, yet still related to her.

Finally, a great text from the *Catechism*: "*God has bound salvation to the sacrament of Baptism, but he himself is not bound by his sacraments*" (1257). God's grace, then, can operate outside the "ordinary means," the visible sacraments of the Church.

Thus salvation *through* Christ and the Church is available to those invincibly ignorant of Christ and the Church. But the faster a person can get to the Church and the sacraments, the better—such channels of God's grace are powerful beyond measure. (Someone can do advanced math and physics without a calculator, but what a hindrance!) For instance, baptism and confirmation impart what is called a sacramental "character," a permanent change in the person's very being, grafting him on to Christ (*CCC* 1272–74). It's like being built, constituted, to receive the fullness of grace.

By the way, these points are central to participated theonomy.

Catholicism is the most user-friendly outlook available: Everyone is included (see *VS* 94), but everyone is ready for more of what they already possess. (Imagine giving a calculator to someone already in love with math and physics.) Quite an impetus for evangelization (see *VS* 106)!

Revelation is obviously central to the moral life! I like the idea that Revelation is Christ himself. We know he is present through Scripture, but what exactly is "Tradition"?

We can begin by asking what Jesus left behind for his followers. He did not leave anything written, however much we might wish he had. Rather he left behind, simply put, a massive impact on his followers (the apogee of which was his resurrection—see *CCC* 638).

Since this impact was not summarized in writing by Christ, it was oral and was handed down orally (*DV* 7; *CCC* 76). Tradition is none other than Christ himself as handed on throughout history. (The Latin root of the word "tradition" means to "carry across.") This oral Tradition continues to be handed down today through the apostolic succession—the pope and college of bishops who guard the deposit of faith from generation to generation.

Early in Christian history, various aspects of Tradition were crystallized in written form by eyewitnesses of Christ—his friends and companions—and close friends of eyewitnesses. In the second century the Magisterium of the Church determined that certain of these writings were inspired by God in a unique way, and these became the canon of the New

Testament. So Scripture is the first crystallization of Tradition. It flows out of Tradition and its canon is chosen within the flow of Tradition (see *DV* 8).

It is logically impossible, then, to claim that Scripture alone is the source of Revelation, since Scripture flows from Tradition. Scripture is a prized portion of Tradition.

Because Scripture is the earliest crystallization, because it is linked to eyewitnesses or close associates of eyewitnesses, and because its inspiration is uniquely under the guidance of the Holy Spirit (*DV* 11), it is given a certain pride of place next to Tradition—its "twin," as it were. So important is Scripture that no truth of Tradition can ever contradict it, and all truths of Tradition are latent within it (see *DV* 9).

Beyond Scripture, Tradition is found in doctrine, in the life of the Church, and in the liturgy (*DV* 8, *CCC* 78, *VS* 109–112). Tradition, understood as this rich mystery of Christ himself carried across the centuries through the successors of the apostles, can now easily be distinguished from traditions with a small "t". Spontaneous and unofficial liturgical acts, methods of personal prayer, various customs, Church art and architecture, all these can be valuable *reflectors* of Tradition, but should not be absolutized.

Why focus on the sources of Revelation in a discussion of moral theology? Because the moral life is the following of Christ, and we have access to this living person in Scripture and Tradition. *VS* signals this connection by starting with a reflection on the scriptural story of the rich young man who encounters Christ.

Using arguments based in the natural law, we can take moral truth and make it accessible on a rational level. But that truth has its ultimate source in Christ, whom we meet in Scripture and Tradition.

See *VS:* 6–11; 109–112

Let's get down to brass tacks. Where does the Magisterium fit into Revelation? Some theologians say that the Magisterium doesn't teach infallibly in the area of morality.

The bearer or carrier of Tradition and Scripture, the apostolic succession, also *interprets* those sources of Revelation at numerous junctures throughout history. The Holy Spirit acts within the teaching authority of the Church (the Magisterium) throughout the ages to guarantee proper interpretation of both Tradition and Scripture (*DV* 10, *CCC* 85). At particular moments in history—ecumenical councils, for example—the apostolic succession takes on the role of interpreter or teacher, and so can be termed the Magisterium from the Latin word for teacher, *magister.*

At those moments, part of Tradition becomes written, analogous to Scripture that crystallizes in written form a portion of ongoing tradition. Perhaps the part of written Tradition with which you are most familiar is the Documents of Vatican II.

What would happen if the task of interpretation were given to individual members of the faithful? There would be innumerable subjective interpretations! It is only reasonable that God would provide a source of interpretation that is objective and reliable.

The scriptural grounding for this view of authority is found in Matthew 16:17-19, where we read that Christ gives the "keys of the kingdom of heaven" to St. Peter. The importance of the apostolic succession, with Peter's successor at its helm, is found throughout the New Testament and is most visibly present in the earliest writings of the Apostolic Fathers in the second century such as Clement of Rome, Ignatius of Antioch, and Irenaeus.

The human beings who make up the Magisterium at any given point in history are by no means immune from mistakes. That's why, for example, John Paul II recently apologized for mistakes made by personnel of the Church in the past. Rather, they are immune *when teaching dogmatically.*

In the midst of so grave a task, they might make imprudent judgments in other respects. They are not necessarily saints. Nor are they by definition good organizers or speakers or public relations agents.

Given such limitations, a variety of "checks" exist within the workings of the Magisterium to prevent abuse of authority. Not everything that is taught by the Magisterium is on the same level; much is within the realm of custom or discipline (little "t" traditions). Then, in the category of doctrine there are various levels of authority. Some of these doctrines have the status of infallibility and require the assent of faith, while others require assent of mind and will (see *LG* 25). And in answer to your other question, yes, some of the former are in the realm of morality.

I'm glad to hear that some moral norms are infallible—but how? Which ones? How do we know? Let me get even more

directly to the point: Lots of people want to know whether the teaching on contraception is infallible. This makes a big difference to them.

This will take some doing, so fasten your seat belts and keep your eyes on the diagram! Vatican II was careful to point out exactly when and where the voice of the Magisterium speaks infallibly. The varying "voices" of the Magisterium are spelled out in *LG* 25. Let's begin with an explanatory outline of that important article, looking to those three places (indicated by asterisks) where the Magisterium speaks infallibly.

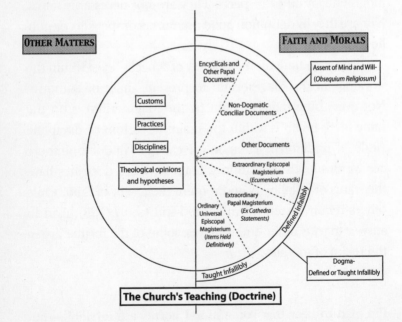

OTHER MATTERS

FAITH AND MORALS

Encyclicals and Other Papal Documents

Assent of Mind and Will- (*Obsequium Religiosum*)

Customs

Practices

Disciplines

Non-Dogmatic Conciliar Documents

Theological opinions and hypotheses

Other Documents

Extraordinary Episcopal Magisterium (*Ecumenical councils*)

Ordinary Universal Episcopal Magisterium (*Items Held Definitively*)

Extraordinary Papal Magisterium (*Ex Cathedra Statements*)

Defined Infallibly

Taught Infallibly

Dogma- Defined or Taught Infallibly

The Church's Teaching (Doctrine)

I. The Extraordinary Magisterium

First, let's distinguish the *extraordinary* Magisterium from the *ordinary* Magisterium. "Extraordinary" and "ordinary" refer to the manner in which a truth is stated, whether or not that truth is infallible. Imagine a parent, on the one hand, regularly reminding children of good manners—an "ordinary" exercise of authority. Then imagine her, on the other hand, writing up a set of guidelines and proclaiming them officially at a special family meeting—an "extraordinary" exercise of authority.

An *ex cathedra* papal statement would be an example of the Magisterium teaching in an extraordinary manner, as would an ecumenical council at which many bishops of the world—the *episcopacy*—are gathered. We could say, then, that the extraordinary Magisterium consists of a *papal* and an *episcopal* dimension. Let's take a closer look at each:[3]

A. The Extraordinary Papal Magisterium***

Notice the triple asterisks! Here, the pope acts alone and speaks *ex cathedra* ("from the chair") in defining a dogma. Sometimes it's a bit of a shock to realize that this has occurred only twice: (1) The Immaculate Conception of Mary was defined in 1854, by Pope Pius IX, and (2) the Assumption of Mary was defined in 1950, by Pope Pius XII. No matter regarding *morality* has been defined in this manner, for reasons we'll examine shortly.

B. The Extraordinary Episcopal Magisterium

1. Bishops gathered in ecumenical councils can define dogmas.* Triple asterisks again. At the twenty-one ecumenical councils held throughout Christian history, certain items have been infallibly defined. When you say the creed at Mass, you are actually reciting an infallible definition originating at the councils of Nicea (325) and Constantinople (381). (It's technically called the Nicene-Constanopolitan Creed—try that tongue twister!) Or consider Chalcedon's (451) definition of the two natures of Christ, or Trent's (1561) definition of the seven sacraments.

One Marian dogma was defined in this manner: The Council of Ephesus, against a heresy called Nestorianism, defined Mary as *Theotokos*, Mother of God. And by the way, no *moral* teachings have been defined in this way. But be patient!

2. Bishops gathered in ecumenical councils can proclaim the gospel and give pastoral directions. Councils also teach many non-infallible matters. It's important to realize that not every pronouncement at an ecumenical council is infallible. Some pronouncements deal with matters of faith and morals, while others are of a disciplinary or prudential nature. In any case, they are not in themselves infallible.

For instance, the majority of documents from Vatican II are of this non-infallible nature. *Dignitatis Humanae* (The Decree on Religious Freedom), for example, rests upon the dogma that the Catholic Church is the true

Church of Christ. But it goes on to speak of political matters, an area on which the Church's infallible authority does not come to bear.

We owe a "religious submission" or a "reverent obedience" (*obsequium religiosum* is the technical term) of mind and will to those non-infallible matters that are nonetheless within the realm of faith and morals. Later we'll say a bit more on what that kind of assent means.

II. The Ordinary Magisterium

A. The ordinary papal Magisterium consists in popes' teaching "authentically," usually in documents such as encyclicals or apostolic exhortations. These documents may contain truths that are taught infallibly, but the documents as a whole are not infallible. Rather, they require the "assent of mind and will" of the faithful (mentioned just above), an assent that is distinct in nature from the "assent of faith" required of items infallibly taught.

Humanae Vitae, for instance, is not an infallible document. It contains ideas that require respectful assent but which, while not being erroneous, may be incomplete or partially flawed. In article 12, however, the pope touches upon a matter that, it can be argued, is infallibly taught: The inseparability of the unitive and procreative dimensions of each conjugal act. Thus the evil of contraception can be said to be taught infallibly.

In sum, non-infallible documents can contain items that are infallibly taught or defined. Now you know how to repond to someone who says "*Humanae Vitae* is not an infallible document, so it's up to us, after considering it, to make up our own minds."

B. The ordinary episcopal magisterium includes bishops teaching non-universally and universally.

1. Non-universally. Non-universal episcopal teaching occurs when bishops teach on items specific to their geographical location. A bishop could teach on his own, as when a single bishop appeals to a state official not to use the death penalty. Or bishops could teach together in episcopal conferences, as when the U.S. bishops promulgated their pastoral letters on war and peace or on the economy. They might refer to items that are infallibly taught or defined, but their teaching on a specific matter is not infallible. Nevertheless, their teaching deserves our mindful attention.

2. Universally.* There it is—the third set of triple asterisks! This is the most important category for our purposes, and we'll treat it in detail shortly. First, let's give it an official name, which is good to memorize: the *ordinary universal episcopal Magisterium*. Got it? Remember the initials: OUEM.

Now for the thumbnail definition, also worth mastering for those who appreciate the Church's guidance in living the good life: When the bishops gathered throughout the world have at some time agreed on a matter of divine revelation, dealing with faith or morals, to be held definitively, such agreement constitutes infallible teaching and is irreversible. This category is especially important because *moral* matters that are taught infallibly belong right here.

In sum, there are a variety of levels on which the Magisterium speaks. Three of these, asterisked in the outline above, constitute infallible teaching.[4]

I took you seriously and have already memorized the key points. The category most important for morality is—are you ready—the *ordinary universal episcopal Magisterium* (OUEM for short). And the definition is this: When (a) all bishops throughout the world, at any particular time in history, have (b) concurred on some matter of faith and morals, and (c) taught it definitively, then that matter is considered to be infallibly *taught.* How did I do?

Your grade is "A+." Note that the OUEM does not *define* infallibly, as would be the case if there were an exercise of the *extraordinary* Magisterium as indicated in the above outline. Rather, it *teaches* infallibly—here, "defined" and "taught" are technical terms. Whether taught infallibly or defined infallibly, the matter is just as infallible.[5]

By analogy, in a classroom a professor might state certain instructions in an extraordinary way by using special means of emphasis. For example, he might carefully *define* on the course syllabus the course requirements or the method of grading. Other items, of equal or even greater importance, might be *taught* in an entirely ordinary way (for example, advice on how to read a challenging book), or because they are such obvious points that they are not stated at all but are taught implicitly (for example, respecting one another's contributions in class).

Same for the Church. She both *defines* certain matters infallibly in an extraordinary way, and *teaches* other matters infallibly in an ordinary way.

Using our example again, imagine the teacher taking his advice on how to read a challenging book, and putting it in writing for all the students. Something taught "infallibly" is now more officially "defined." So also with the Church's infallible teaching.

Matters that are defined infallibly usually have been taught infallibly prior to the extraordinary definition. Often what causes a matter to be raised to the level of an infallible definition is some type of crisis requiring a more official definition. It is always a question of prudence as to whether or not to define a matter that is already infallibly taught by the ordinary universal episcopal Magisterium. (There's that mouthful again—by now, though, you have it down cold.)

The encyclical *Evangelium Vitae* could have been the context within which the pope defined infallibly the Church's teaching on the sanctity of human life, on abortion, and on euthanasia. Instead, the pope wisely used the encyclical to point out, in the midst of carefully reasoned argumentation, that these matters are already taught infallibly by the ordinary universal episcopal Magisterium. What would happen if several bishops were to teach otherwise? They themselves would stand in conflict with the Tradition, and in a sense would be standing outside the apostolic Tradition at least on a particular issue. We would not agree with their dissenting position, but as members of the apostolic succession they still guard the deposit of faith in all other respects.

Now that it's clear that some moral matters are taught infallibly, can we consider some specific examples?

Let's use *Evangelium Vitae*. That encyclical dealt with three infallible teachings: the sanctity of human life (57), the evil of abortion (62), and the evil of euthanasia (65). The pope used the same language for each of the three; here let's consider the argument regarding the sanctity of life:

> Faced with the progressive weakening in individual consciences and in society of the sense of the absolute and grave moral illicitness of the direct taking of all innocent human life, especially in its beginning and at its end, the Church's Magisterium has spoken out with increasing frequency in defense of the sacredness and inviolability of human life. The Papal Magisterium, particularly insistent in this regard, has always been seconded by that of the Bishops, with numerous and comprehensive doctrinal and pastoral documents issued either by Episcopal Conferences or by individual bishops. The Second Vatican Council also addressed this matter forcefully, in a brief but incisive passage [the reference is to *GS* 27].

Test yourself: Find the spot where the text has made reference to the ordinary papal Magisterium, and recall that it is not infallible in and of itself. Then find the spot where the text references the non-universal episcopal Magisterium, also not infallible in and of itself. The point is that popes and bishops have consistently and definitively spoken out in defense of the sanctity of life.

Against this backdrop, we can go on to determine whether this matter—the inviolable sanctity of human life—might be infallibly taught by the ordinary universal episcopal Magisterium. Look at the next part of the text. The pope is not defining infallibly, but rather is confirming that this matter is already taught infallibly by the ordinary universal episcopal Magisterium:

> Therefore, by the authority which Christ conferred upon Peter and his successors, and in communion with the bishops of the Catholic Church, *I confirm that the direct and voluntary killing of an innocent human being is always gravely immoral.* This doctrine, based upon that unwritten law which man, in the light of reason, finds in his own heart (see Rom 2:14-15) is reaffirmed by Sacred Scripture, transmitted by the Tradition of the Church, and taught by the ordinary and universal Magisterium [a reference is then made to *LG* 25].

We stand reminded! This is a clear statement (a reminder) that these moral matters are taught (not defined) infallibly. Likewise, any other moral matters that have infallible status are taught, not defined, infallibly by the ordinary universal episcopal Magisterium.

Some examples? Consider those teachings rooted in the nature of the conjugal act as unitive and procreative, such as the teachings against homosexual acts, adultery and fornication, contraception and sterilization, auto-eroticism, and certain new birth technologies. And don't forget—such prohibitions are really in the service of a positive norm: Respect the dignity of the human person. By the way, note the clear teaching in the above text about the natural law, and the reaffirmation of certain truths of the natural law by the twin sources of Revelation—a nice re-cap of some of our main themes.

Given this clearly infallible teaching on moral matters, how can theologians claim that there exists no infallible teaching on morality?

Let's outline and then unmask their argument.[6]

(a) No matters of morality, they claim, have ever been defined infallibly by the Magisterium.

(b) Therefore, all matters of morality are in the realm of fallible teachings that do not demand our assent of faith, but rather a lesser assent.

(c) Such teachings have changed in the past. For instance, the teaching that condemned religious liberty was not infallible, and it changed at Vatican II.

(d) We are in the midst of another such change regarding the issue of contraception and other related issues. So while giving due respect to the Magisterium, it is legitimate to dissent from these teachings.

Ready to unmask? See if you can explain why points (a) and (b) are correct in what they state, but omit something really important. (Answer: True enough, matters of morality have not been *defined* infallibly, but they have been *taught* infallibly. Yes, one whole category of infallible teaching is conveniently ignored in this argument!)

Now for a more challenging item: Why is point (c) erroneous? (Answer: Because those moral matters infallibly taught have *not* been changed, and the fact that non-infallible matters such as religious liberty have changed is not a problem precisely because such teaching belong in a different category, demanding a different type of assent.)

Finally, point (d) is a false conclusion because some of its premises are false, irrelevant, or incomplete.

Why can't all the truths of the faith be presented with the same degree of absolute clarity? For example, why not take the whole *Catechism* and define it infallibly?

While in one sense it might be beneficial for everything to be clear cut, it would also be somewhat inappropriate. In no other area of human life do we learn such complex matters in such a simple, clear-cut way. We learn gradually, and only over time arrive at a certain clarity.

God does not short-circuit the "laws" of learning. Jesus himself did not leave behind a crystal-clear guidebook of infallible teachings, but rather gave the truth over to the Church to hand on (Tradition) with the promise of guidance by the Holy Spirit. In this Tradition, not all truths have the same status—the same as in any other skill you master.

Some truths of faith and morals are infallible doctrines demanding assent of faith. Others demand a different kind of assent, the assent of mind and will. Still other truths are not in the realm of faith and morals at all (customs, practices, disciplines, and such).

An analogy might show the appropriateness of such categories. Imagine putting yourself in the care of a doctor who, while a general practitioner, also happens to have unique expertise in one particular area such as allergy problems. When you take his advice on a variety of different problems, you are aware that different pieces of advice are given with different kinds of authority.

What he says to you about your allergies might be likened to an infallible truth to which you give a whole-hearted assent (assent of faith). Meanwhile, his advice on your painful knee (remember, it kept you from ascending that mountain peak?) is also taken seriously, but not with the same high degree of assent. Still, you have put yourself in his care, and you take his advice as a whole. (I'll do whatever you say, Doc!)

Likewise, the Church teaches some matters infallibly and other matters with lesser degrees of certitude. You put your soul in her care and follow her teachings ("Lord, to whom else can we go?") even while the type of assent given to different types of teachings may vary. A Catholic ought not spend too much time worrying about these different degrees of assent—that is one reason why various documents of the Magisterium, including VS[7] and the *Catechism*, do not dwell on these distinctions too much.

Let's avoid a minimalist attitude that too anxiously seeks out those items that are infallible. Instead, let's embrace the whole truth, as articulated in the *Catechism*, even though these truths are taught with differing degrees of authority.[8]

It makes a lot of sense why there are different kinds of teachings. But why not take the most important kind—the infallible ones—and have the pope clearly define all these things once and for all? Why is there any need for the somewhat hazy category of the ordinary universal episcopal Magisterium?

How would non-Catholics around the world react? Remember that the Church sees her teaching on moral matters as knowable by *everyone* through the natural law, to which we all have access by use of reason alone, without the aid of Revelation. When the Church teaches that homosexual activity is wrong, this teaching is true for everyone. Everyone, Catholic or not, is expected to follow this truth, not because the Church teaches it, but because the natural law, written on everyone's heart by the Creator, teaches it.

Imagine if the Church were to define such teachings in an extraordinary way—a sudden series of *ex cathedra* statements, for example? Your secularist friend would say: "You Catholics had better adhere to that, but as for myself, I prefer to think independently."

Now, imagine the extraordinary Magisterium defining only a few matters of morality—abortion, for instance. Imagine one of your Catholic friends saying, "I sure am glad some of those other teachings (on contraception, on homosexual acts) were left undefined. In a word, it seems prudent to reserve matters of morality to the ordinary universal episcopal Magisterium.

John Paul II clearly has used a strategy that allows the universal Church to be received as universally as possible. There is reason to hope that in time many of those who are alienated will once again embrace the full apostolic tradition. By refraining from *ex cathedra* statements, the pope may have intended to give some "breathing space" to those who have difficulty receiving the teaching, thereby giving the Church as a whole more time to absorb it.[9]

Note how the pope's approach avoids both the extreme of autonomy (avoiding teaching on tough issues) and the extreme of heteronomy (laying down the law hard and cold). The Magisterium of John Paul II exemplifies participated theonomy.

Speaking of autonomy, heteronomy, and participated theonomy, observe a fascinating point about authority: Many people today shirk from the very idea of authority, thinking of it as an affront to their autonomy. They see the very idea of authority as heteronomous, as an arbitary imposition. But they are simply substituting one arbitrary authority (their concept of a rigid tyrant telling them what to do) for another arbitrary authority (themselves).

You can't get rid of authority! If you are told in a heated discussion that you are too rigid and obsessed with authority figures such as the pope, you might ask, "On whose authority do you claim that there are no ultimate authorities for humanity?" In a word, it is part and parcel of humanity to seek authority, simply because we are not gods, and our own powers of insight and judgment are limited.

So the real question is not whether authority is good or bad, but rather, whose authority it is most reasonable and prudent to follow. Which authority is genuinely friendly to humanity? Which authority helps us avoid the extremes of autonomy and heteronomy? When it comes to matters concerning our final eternal destiny, you want to be doubly sure you get the right authority.

Read *VS:* 109–117. *Numerous texts in this section place the authority of the church within the ambit of participated theonomy. Please see the web site as well.*
Study *CCC:* 2032–46.

SIX

DISORDERED GOODS: THE MYSTERY OF SIN

It seems as though the moment we mention the word *sin*, we are immediately accused of being judgmental and intolerant. Critics are quick to cite Jesus' command not to judge. How do we navigate through such murky waters?

The very word "sin" can easily conjure up a heteronomous understanding of the moral life, in which life is set up by a fearsome God, with plenty of traps into which we might fall, sending us to eternal damnation. In reaction, many revisionist thinkers have gone to the autonomous extreme of virtually denying the existence of sin. The solution found in *VS* is to understand sin in the context of participated theonomy.

Consider this analogy. We only enjoy a piece of music when it is properly ordered—everything in tune, everyone playing the right notes, just the right way, together. When something is out of order (there is a "lack of due order"), we appreciate the person who fixes it—the conductor—with a call for more careful tuning, for more accurate rhythm, or for one instrument to be quieter and another louder.

No one is interested in *placing blame* on anyone—that's a separate issue. Rather, proper order is needed so that the audience, and the musicians themselves, can be truly happy. So the conductor who fixes the problem must not be afraid to be very direct about what constitutes lack of due order, and very direct about how to fix it. Again, the conductor isn't first interested in *blaming* (assigning culpability to) one musician or another, but in keeping the whole symphony *on track*.

In a similar way, when Christ tells us about sin, he is not primarily interested in assigning blame. He wants our happiness: "Go and sin no more," he repeatedly tells people. They repent, reform, and go away *healthy*.

When Christ says, "I forgive you" (sacramentally, through the priest), these are the happiest words imaginable, and they could not be spoken unless the individual has first been pointed in the right direction. *Sin* is a very friendly reminder to us about what constitutes the wrong direction, or lack of due order. That is why sin is called, as we noted earlier, a *privation*. It prevents us from being aligned with true happiness—which comes from the delight in being allowed to *participate* in God's proper order (*theonomy*).

Let me try to make a connection here. An "out of order act" would be a *malum*, right? In your analogy, this would be like a wrong note, or an out-of-tune instrument. Then comes the question of whether an individual is to *blame* for a bad act, and that would be a *culpa*. Am I right? And does the word "sin" apply to both?

One-hundred-percent right, and here's how the word "sin" works. We can refer to certain *actions* as sins, and when we do, we mean they are the kinds of acts that, if committed freely and knowingly, would be true sins *for us* (*culpa*).

When looking only at the action itself, aside from our personal involvement, we are looking at a *malum*. We can also use the term *material sin,* meaning that the "matter" or "stuff" of the act is disordered. When we "plug ourselves in" to that act, as free and knowledgeable agents, then we are looking at a *culpa.* We can then also use the term *formal sin*—an individual person "gets herself stuck in" the matter, "infuses" the matter, in*forms* the matter.

For example, an act of fornication, or an act of theft, is materially sinful. These are the kinds of acts that, if done freely and knowingly, would also be formally sinful—sins *for us* (*culpa*).

Note the conditions here: "done freely and knowingly." For an act to be *formally sinful,* that is, for an person's wrong act (*malum*) to be done culpably, those conditions must be met—and of course the act itself has to be an evil act. A common way for theologians to put this is that three conditions have to be met:

1. The act itself must be evil, rather than good or neutral.
2. The agent must intend the act rather than being forced to do it (explicitly or more subtly).
3. The agent must know that the act is evil.

These conditions remind us that the claim that a particular act is evil (abortion, for example) is not a claim that the agent has sinned.[1] A *malum* is not always a *culpa.* Act and agent must be kept distinct. Again, to speak of the act as evil is to speak of *material* sin, while to speak of the agent culpably doing that act is to speak of *formal* sin.

When Christ tells us not to judge, he means we are not to judge the *blameworthiness* of the agent. On the other hand, we are obligated to judge some acts as evil. For instance, homosexual acts can be judged as evil, but the homosexual person engaging in the act is not to be judged at all. And that person's homosexual *condition*, while a disorder, is by no means morally evil—in fact, the presence of this condition would be a central factor in affecting that person's responsibility for a homosexual act.

Today, "being judgmental" is considered an undesirable personality trait. But note that we cannot help but make judgments. Even the oft-heard command "Don't be judgmental" itself reflects a judgment. So it is better to admit that making judgments is necessary, and then to discern carefully which kinds of judgments are appropriate and which aren't. Judgments of individuals are never appropriate, and amount to another sin—that of pride.

I've seen some people get preoccupied with figuring out which sins fit into which category—mortal and venial. It's a kind of "what can I get away with" legalism. A friend told me he only goes to confession when he thinks he's committed a mortal sin. What can I say to my friend?

If you have a heteronomous understanding of sin, it's rather natural to keep those "rigid demands" as limited as possible— the rich young man who came to Jesus wanted to keep the commandments, and no more. Aside from a short list of absolute prohibitions, you carve out as much autonomy as possible! This is in fact a great example of how autonomy and heteronomy, both equally arbitrary, can appear simultaneously.

After all, they are flip sides of the same arbitrary coin.

To keep the Catholic doctrine about sin in the context of participated theonomy, first recall the central place of grace in the moral life, God's love poured into our hearts (Rom 5:5). By this grace we are made partakers in the very life of God himself. We are wayfarers on a journey toward the beatific vision, where we will be fully immersed in or encompassed by that grace.

It is this grace—as a final goal and as a reality already inhering in us—that is threatened by sin. So it is not a matter of legalistic preoccupation with gradations of sin. All sin is a hindrance to reaching the beatific vision.

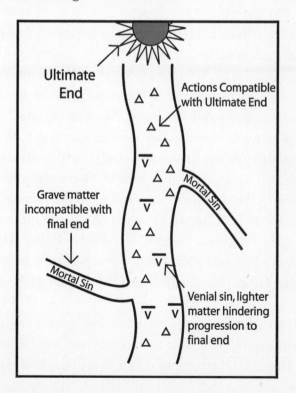

It is as if you were traveling down a winding river toward the port; on the way are many adjoining rivers, and also many minor obstacles. As you chart your course, your final goal is to reach port; all your more immediate goals are subordinate to that final goal. The more immediate goals of avoiding an obstacle, or of resisting the current that might lead you down an adjoining river, are pursued because of the final goal.

So, too, in the moral life. All more immediate goals are pursued in light of the final goal of union with God. And we must add that there is an astonishing phenomenon about this journey. The Person toward whom we are headed is right next to us, and in fact right *inside* us, as we make our way. Our goal is truly a *friendly* goal!

Put in Trinitarian terms, as we are headed toward the Father, the Son walks with us and the Spirit abides in us. So we can meet all the challenges and obstacles along the way because we are not alone. The Trinitarian God, our final end, dwells in us, and with his grace all things are possible.

Now let's continue the analogy with attention to the mortal/venial distinction. Venial sin would be analogous to getting temporarily caught in some obstacle: "It impedes the soul's progress in the exercise of the virtues and the practice of the moral good" (*CCC* 1863). However, we remain on our basic path toward our final destiny: "Venial sin does not break the covenant with God" (*CCC* 1863). Some particular good is out of order, but not in such a way that the ultimate highest good, God himself, is denied.

Mortal sin, on the other hand, is like getting caught in a whole different stream that takes us an entirely different direction. Mortal sin destroys our orientation to our final goal. *The person in mortal sin has a new ultimate end!* "[Mortal sin] turns man away from God, who is his ultimate end and his beatitude, by preferring an inferior good to him" (*CCC* 1855).

Not only is that inferior good not properly ordered (as with venial sin). It has actually become the person's new ultimate end. In turn, God, the highest good, gets turned into a lower good, subordinate to our new god.

This is why mortal sinners still might claim that they have not rejected God. Well, God may be there, but no longer as the highest good. Rather, he is now one good alongside others.

To say he is one good alongside others is to say that he is not God! That's why mortal sin is so serious: By "demoting" God to a lower good, we deny the true God. And just as bad, that new god will never match the true God in satisfying us.

The new god, be it pleasure, prestige, or power, will be *insatiable* and will drain every last bit of happiness out of us. So Christ's warning us about this through the Church is far from a heteronomous scare tactic. It is a sign of true friendship.

And a true friend will help out when you get off course. How do the two types of sin get fixed?

If you don't mind the river analogy again, imagine actually heading down a new, adjoining stream. You might decide that it was a very unwise choice that headed you in a totally wrong direction. You might think, *Turn around!*

But it will be impossible for you to do this on your own. The current is leading you away. The original current of the river, orienting you to your true goal, is missing (a serious privation).

You need someone to pick up your boat and deliver it back to the original course.

Likewise with mortal sin. By "attacking the vital principle within us—that is, charity—[it] necessitates a new initiative of God's mercy and a conversion of heart" (*CCC* 1856). Only God can repair this damage. He always takes the initiative—a steadfast, enduring invitation to turn back to him.

Venial sin inhibits the journey to the final goal but is not permanent. As with an undue delay on the river journey, when the sin stops we can seek forgiveness and be on our way. Since we still possess God's grace within us, we possess that power, an intrinsic principle, by which a venial sin is pardoned.

The word *venial* comes from the Latin *venia*, a noun meaning "pardon" or "acquittal." That which allows pardon to occur is already inhering within us as grace.[2]

If venial sin isn't so drastic—we still have God's life dwelling in us—why worry about it too much? And doesn't the Church require that only mortal sins be confessed?

Confessing mortal sins once a year is the *very* bare minimum. Remember that great text in *VS* 52 that tells us there is a "lower limit" beneath which we should not go? Christ through the Church reminds us of that lower limit, but there is so much more for us to participate in. *VS* 52 says next that there is no upper limit in the moral life—the life of virtue is where the real action is.

We grow in virtue by an honest attentiveness to disordered

parts of our life, however small. Besides, "deliberate and unrepented venial sin disposes us little by little to commit mortal sin" (*CCC* 1863). If various goods are allowed to remain slightly disordered, the way is paved for some such good to assert itself so boldly that it becomes the ultimate good. Probably many mortal sins started with a long and consistent pattern of venial sin.

While we're on the topic, consider a couple more fascinating parts of the mortal/venial distinction. For a sin to be mortal the "matter" must be grave—robbing a bank as opposed to pocketing a dollar that technically isn't yours. In many cases the matter might be grave—so it's a mortal sin *materially*—but the circumstances and intent of the agent affect the freedom and knowledge with which the act is done, making the material mortal sin into a venial sin. Consider evil acts done in wartime, but under severe pressure from a ruthless dictator. You could put it this way: acts that are mortal materially might well be venial formally. (Remember that "formally" has to do with how the material act actually affects, or "forms," a particular agent, while "materially" considers the act objectively, apart from that particular agent.)

Could an act that is venial materially (stealing a penny) ever become mortal formally (the scrupulous agent thinks it's mortal)? Impossible—there must be grave matter for there to be mortal sin. What if an agent mistakenly *thinks* that a *good or neutral act* is mortally sinful (again, this happens often to scrupulous people)? Same thing—unless the matter is grave, it can't be a mortal sin, materially or formally, though there could be formal venial sin in such an instance (this is the case discussed in chapter 1 of the false and bad conscience.) An example: a couple might erroneously think that they ought to have as many children as physically possible (false conscience) and then they feel guilty (bad conscience) of serious sin as they use NFP in limiting family size.

These distinctions are incredibly helpful. But why do some of my non-Catholic friends so dislike the mortal/venial distinction?

They'll be better friends than ever when you tell them what I'm about to tell you. But first a quick game: I'll lead you through a series of supposedly logical steps, and you try to find the error.

Imagine yourself offending someone such as your boss at work. You can rather easily repair the damage by working doubly hard. Now, you get a job with the CEO. You're on pins and needles, because the high dignity of this person means that even a little mistake would be a disaster.

Now transfer your thinking to God, who is infinite. Any offense against him is an *infinite* disaster, something really deadly. Therefore all sin is mortal. Since we do in fact sin, all is lost—you might say we *are* sin. Put otherwise, we are all utterly depraved.

To its credit, this view is intent on upholding God's sovereignty. If an offense against God can be merely venial, then he might appear to be more like your boss—not totally sovereign. From a Catholic view, however, such a view betrays a heteronomous notion of sovereignty. God is then like the angry parent who goes into a rage at his children's slightest offense. Such a father may be sovereign, but he is a sovereign tyrant who cannot distinguish between less grievous (venial) human failings of his children, and their truly serious offenses.

Instead, locate God's sovereignty in his powerful and loving desire to pour his very self into us. So powerful is this divine life that it is not easily dispelled—you can't easily "budge" it. Our minor rebellions (venial sins) are *no match* for this grace. So God's sovereignty is upheld when it comes to the doctrine of venial sin.

What else can a truly sovereign God do? He gives us that supreme gift by which we are made in his image—freedom. And if this is a genuine freedom, it must have the capacity to *reject our ultimate end.*

Mortal sin is that rejection. So the doctrine about mortal sin upholds God's sovereignty by pointing to the heights of the gift of freedom. Now recall: The power of God's grace, and the power of the gift of freedom, are both essential parts of participated theonomy.

Notice that the anthropology of some Christian traditions does not allow for this indwelling sanctifying grace or for our full freedom. Rather, in their view God's grace is imputed to us, covering our depravity, and our full freedom is lost with original sin. The mortal/venial distinction, so important for participated theonomy, vanishes with this heteronomous view.

It's important to recognize that Catholics themselves are partly to blame for the "overreach" to God's sovereignty characteristic of some Christian traditions. Catholic practice can deteriorate into a "works righteousness" in which we imagine, or at least convey that we imagine, that we by ourselves contribute a good deal to our salvation. Recall the rich young man, content with his own rigorous attention to the commandments but unwilling to throw himself into the full moral life of grace and virtue. Or think of those who, like the Pharisees criticized by Christ, work hard at practicing all the right rituals, earning their way into heaven.

The understandable reaction against that "works-centered" salvation is to emphasize the immense gap between humanity and a sovereign God who alone can save us. That's a good instinct, because only God's grace can save us, but it becomes heteronomous rather quickly. Given the immense gap, you salvage God's sovereignty but end up with human depravity.

Another mistake to which Catholics are prone is scrupulosity. That's the tendency to treat minor faults (a perpetually messy desk or kitchen) or even idiosyncracies as sins; to treat uninvited impure thoughts (of, say, less than ten seconds) as sins; to treat venial sins as if they were mortal sins; and to be unduly fearful of damnation when you are in fact living the sacramental life. Like those who think that a minor sin can "budge" God's indwelling presence, scrupulous people think their minor faults and venial sins might budge God's grace. It's an unintended arrogance to think that God's grace is that easily manipulated.

Participated theonomy—you guessed it—has it all, and your non-Catholic friends (and scrupulous Catholic friends) will be intrigued by it at least. God is totally sovereign, but he exhibits the heights of his sovereign power by infusing his own life into us, allowing us to participate in his Trinitarian life, while retaining our full freedom. There is no view of the human person, no *anthropology*, more noble than that.

I wandered into a really difficult part of *VS*—articles 65–70— which talks about the "fundamental option." It seemed as if the pope went back and forth—positive and negative—in discussing this theory. I think I'm missing out on something really intriguing and really important. Can you explain what the "fundamental option" is?

The *fundamental option* theory is a great way to understand the "mystery of iniquity"—sin. Unfortunately the theory has been badly misused by revisionist theologians. But let's deal with the bright side first.

At the very depths of our being we do make a basic choice for or against God, and this ultimate choice is called the "fundamental option." *VS* 66 notes that Scripture and Tradition attest to the idea that there is a deep core aspect of the self which the Bible calls the "heart." This level of the self is distinct from, though closely connected to, the more surface level at which our concrete moral activity takes place.

A mortal sin drastically affects this fundamental option, turning us away from God, while a venial sin leaves our fundamental option toward God intact. It should be noted that the Church's dogmatic heritage, while definitively teaching that mortal and venial sin exist as a threat to charity (God's grace in us), does not teach precisely how they affect charity. The fundamental option theory exists not as a dogma but as a theological hypothesis about the workings of sin in the core of our being.[3]

The theory, with its distinction between the two levels of the self, is helpful for understanding our relationship with God. The two levels have technical names—the *transcendental* level is the core part of the self, and the *categorical* level is the day-to-day surface part.[4] The two levels are best explained with an analogy from human relationships.

If you try to explain why you really love someone, you list all sorts of interesting things on the surface level but finally say that none of those things allow a clear insight into the love itself, which lies much deeper. The surface level manifests the deeper level, but is distinct from it. Our relationship with God works analogously.

A fascinating exercise reveals the nature of this inner mystery. In every act of knowing or willing, there is a subjective and an objective component, that is, a subject who does the knowing—you yourself—and the object that is known. So if you look out the window and say, "That is a tree," *you* are the subject, and the *tree* is the object.

Now think of yourself acting—say, the act of reading this book, or the act of donating money to charity. You are the subject, and the object is the particular act.

Next, I ask you this: What do you know about the inner core of your being? Think a moment, then take this quiz: Name (1) the object and (2) the subject, in that act of knowing.

Answer: (1) The inner core of your being becomes the object of knowledge. (2) The subject has to be the very inner core of your being that you were trying to objectify! Needless to say, that is impossible.

If you try to look at your inner self, it is your own inner self that is doing the looking! Otherwise put, if you wish to consider your self as the object of knowing, the self automatically escapes being objectified and remains the subject! (By the way, the quiz grade doesn't count, since the question is unanswerable!)

For this reason, the self always evades full objectification and full knowledge. It remains a mystery. It is that which does the objectifying, but which itself can never be objectified.

What other being that you know also remains a mystery and cannot be objectified? God! (That's why his answer to Moses' request for his name was "I am who I am.")[5] Through sanctifying grace, this absolute mystery of God, fully transcendent, is present in the mystery of the self.

These two mysteries can converge, even though they remain distinct. The life of sanctifying grace within the self is just this convergence. So St. Paul can say, "It is no longer I who live, but Christ who lives in me" (Gal 2:20).

Some revisionist thinkers conclude that the mystery of the self and the mystery of God, since they evade objectification, become vague entities about which nothing definitive can be said; all we know are vague approximations. The reality, however, is that very definite things *can* be said—from knowledge by both reason and Revelation—about the mystery of the self and the mystery of God. But these definite truths never exhaust the mystery of the self and the mystery of God. They never turn God or the self into objects.

The dogmatic statements of the Church's heritage are, then, accurate windows to the transcendent mysteries of the self and God. Of concern in moral theology is that we can know that certain acts destroy the life of grace in us. We cannot somehow "get inside" the mystery of the self to see this happen (as we have shown, the self cannot be looked at as an object) any more than we can get inside the mystery of God or the mystery of grace dwelling in us. But we can have objectively valid knowledge about the inner workings of grace in the soul.

Christ, working in and through Catholic doctrine, gives us this clear knowledge. When a person commits an act that is taught by the Church to be sinful, that person *sees a manifestation of his or her inner life,* an external sign of what is happening at the core of that person's being. That's why it is so important to be vigilant over our concrete actions. They are like windows through which we get a glimpse of what is happening in our inmost being. Our own feelings and inclinations, our own *experience,* will not necessarily reveal to us the deepest and most important self-knowledge.[6]

The fundamental option theory helps explain a variety of phenomena. For example, it explains why people in a state of mortal sin often can't express why they turned from God, any more than Adam and Eve had a good answer when they committed the first mortal sin in the garden. It's called the mystery of iniquity.

It also explains why a person in a state of grace ordinarily won't fall into mortal sin. At the core level, one is grafted onto God, and day-to-day acts will flow from that fundamental option.

Finally, it demonstrates the importance of regular examination of conscience. Our point of access to what is going on at the core level is our day-to-day action, and so it is important to be vigilant toward that action, always watching for signs that something might be awry in our friendship with God.

Sounds like a really useful theory! But you said it got misused—let me take a guess. A friend of mine went to the sacrament of penance and confessed a mortal sin. The priest apparently asked my friend if she still loved God. She said she

did. The priest said it wasn't a mortal sin so long as you have made a fundamental choice to love God. Is that the misused fundamental option theory at work?

Yes. That priest was affected by some contemporary revisionist theologians who have misused the distinction between the two levels of the self, toward the end of virtually denying the possibility of mortal sin.[7] They claim that our concrete acts don't really affect our inner core.

According to these theologians, the only way you could mortally sin is if you really intended to hate and despise God. The misuse of the category "fundamental option," which might be termed the "radical fundamental option theory," is manifested in assertions such as the following: Don't worry whether a particular act is a mortal sin; rather, ask whether there exists, in the midst of the action, a sincere love of God and neighbor. The quality and "authenticity" of our character and the sincerity of our relationships are more important than isolated actions we perform.

In the "radical fundamental option theory," mortal sin becomes virtually non-existent. The category "mortal sin" then turns into "serious sin" or "grave sin." After all, most people do not engage in sinful actions with the direct intent of despising God.

Recall again the "battle of the goods": Even in a mortal sin we are choosing something good, but with total lack of order in relation to the highest good. With mortal sin, we take a created good and make it into the highest good—that for which we will do anything. God is still treated as a good—but he has been demoted to one good alongside others.

So, to use your example, when the priest asked, "Do you still love God?" the answer will of course be yes. The better question is this: "Are you treating God as the highest good in your life—the One for whom you will do anything, the One to whom you give ultimate allegiance?"

According to the Catholic tradition, a mortal sin, done knowingly and freely, is a visible symbol or indication that at the very core of his or her being a person has decided to give ultimate allegiance to some good other than God. Again, this happens at the core of the person's being without an explicit intent to hurt God. It is analogous to a marriage in which something has gone seriously awry, and the husband says, "I didn't mean to hurt you." Of course he didn't mean to hurt her, but he did, and ruptured the relationship in a serious way. He can't rationalize his way around it.

It is unequivocally stated in *VS* 65–70 (especially 67) that the misuse of the fundamental option theory is incompatible with the Church's understanding of sin. The Church's clear teaching also appeared earlier in *Persona Humana* (*Declaration on Sexual Ethics*):

There are those who go as far as to affirm that mortal sin, which causes separation from God, only exists in the formal refusal directly opposed to God's call, or in that selfishness which completely and deliberately closes itself to the love of neighbor.... According to the Church's teaching, mortal sin, which is opposed to God, does not consist only in formal and direct resistance to the commandment of charity. It is equally to be found in this opposition to authentic love which is included in every deliberate transgression, in serious matter, of each of the moral laws (10).

The radical version of the theory is attractive to many because it has the appearance of compassion. Imagine a practicing homosexual person, or an adulterer, asking a priest if he can still consider himself Catholic. He says that he feels a deep love for God and can't understand why God would not want him to receive the Eucharist, much less how God could ever condemn him, especially given his sincere effort to lead a good life.

The priest could be tempted to tell the man that due to the complexity of his situation (a strong homosexual drive, or a shrewish wife) and due to his sincerity, he need not worry—after all, God is a loving God. Or imagine a contracepting couple, or a businessman doing shady dealings. It's easy to convince yourself that God won't reject you because you're doing the best you can in a tough situation, and because your sincerity is unquestionable.

But such a view manifests a false compassion that in the end makes life more miserable than ever. We can never be truly free until we are working towards aligning ourselves with the truth, which always, for all of us, involves great moral challenges. True compassion would involve honesty about the possibility of mortal sin, coupled with Christ's mercy and offer of forgiveness. True compassion helps people progress on the trajectory of holiness, toward their ultimate beatific end. The radical fundamental option theory too easily provides false justification for abandoning that trajectory.

Read *VS*: 65–70
Study *CCC*: 1846–69

I have a hunch that there is some resemblance between the radical version of the fundamental option and some non-Catholic views of sin and salvation. Am I on target?

The radical fundamental option theory moves toward—and then beyond—the position of some of the Protestant reformers. For them, our actions—in the realm of "works"—cannot affect our status before God. As essentially depraved, we cannot do anything that might merit salvation.

In this view, God, through the redemptive work of Christ, covers over our inherent sinfulness and justifies us. After justification, we ought to strive to lead virtuous lives, but our salvation is not dependent on virtue. Just as in the radical fundamental option theory, none of our concrete moral acts, then, can touch or affect our fundamental status before God, our fundamental option for or against him.

Instead of talking about human depravity, radical theorists use the psychologized secular equivalent, "complexity." And instead of "faith alone," substitute "sincerity" (which includes "tolerance"). Either way, the path to salvation is disconnected from moral endeavor.

But there remains a basic difference between the Reformers' view and the radical fundamental option. For the former, our fundamental status is ontologically depraved and corrupt, and simultaneously covered by God's justifying grace through Christ. For the latter, our fundamental status is essentially good—a denial of original sin.

While this fundamental goodness is at first sight compatible with Catholic anthropology, it is flawed by a psychologized view of goodness that fails to recognize properly our concupiscence—our capacity to act contrary to our natures that have been healed by God's grace (see *VS* 103). The Reformers at least recognized sin, though going to the extreme position that we *are* sin (depravity) even after Christ's redemption. The radical fundamental option theorists ignore the concupiscence that accompanies our healed natures (substituting the complexity of human life) and our capacity to follow the concupiscent tendency in a mortal way.

Christ has not only restored for us the gift of supernatural, sanctifying grace. With that same grace he has healed our natures, making it possible to live virtuously. It is a perennial temptation to affirm the reality of grace, yet not to allow it the possibility of healing our natures.

Some of the Protestant reformers succumbed to this tendency (in their claim that we are simultaneously saved and depraved), and likewise the radical fundamental option theorists. In so doing, the full power of the redemption is minimized. In what is perhaps the most important text in *VS*, John Paul II, quoting from a 1984 papal address on responsible parenthood, reminds us of the power of redemptive grace:

> *Only in the mystery of Christ's Redemption do we discover the "concrete" possibilities of man.* It would be a very serious error to conclude ... that the Church's teaching is essentially only an "ideal" which must then be adapted, proportioned, graduated to the so-called concrete possibilities of man, according to a "balancing of the goods in question." But what are the "concrete possibilities of man?" And of *which* man are we speaking? Of man *dominated* by lust or man *redeemed* by Christ? This is what is at

stake: the *reality* of Christ's redemption. *Christ has redeemed us!* This means that he has given us the possibility of realizing *the entire* truth of our being; he has set our freedom free from the *domination* of concupiscence. And if redeemed man still sins, this is not due to an imperfection of Christ's redemptive act, but to man's will not to avail himself of the grace which flows from that act ... the man who, though he has fallen into sin, can always obtain pardon and enjoy the presence of the Holy Spirit (103).

At the conclusion of the encyclical, the pope makes this same point from Mary's perspective: "Nor does she permit sinful man to be deceived by those who claim to love him by justifying his sin, for she knows that the sacrifice of Christ her Son would thus be emptied of its power." Christ's redemption restores the fullness of grace, as it was "in the beginning" (see *VS* 22.2 and 53.2)

It's interesting to hear that the radical theory "psychologizes" Christianity. So many people seem to have substituted psychological theories, with a big emphasis on self-esteem, for religion. Is psychology incompatible with Christianity?

The radical fundamental option theory easily falls prey to a contemporary error that we might label "psychologism" (which should not be in the least confused with psychology itself, which, when properly used, is fully compatible with Christian faith).[8] That error is this: the notion that as long as we try hard and are sincere, we are OK. We ought not feel guilt about one or another act as long as our intentions were sincere.

This brand of psychologism suggests that the ultimate goal of personal health and wholeness is a good sense of "self-esteem." Too often, it is claimed, guilt gets in the way of such esteem, and we would be better off shedding such feelings.[9] (Note that the focus on self-esteem is not a focus on something bad, but a misalignment of something good. Self-esteem as an out-of-due-order good omits fidelity to the bedrock of moral norms necessary for *genuine* self-esteem, the self-esteem that is the fruit of living in fidelity to the truth, in proper alignment with the ultimate end.[10])

Guilt usually results from the suspicion that God does not approve of some action. Note how the radical fundamental option theory alleviates such guilt: It teaches that so long as a person does not hold God in contempt, and sincerely tries to do what seems best in a given situation, God will not disapprove. To put it in the technical terms from our study of conscience, the good/bad conscience is emphasized to the near exclusion of the true/false conscience.

Guilt, however, can be a friend to the conscience,[11] for when understood properly, it reminds us that our moral life is amiss. Such ""real" or "objective" guilt lets us know that our moral life is not properly ordered. So, rather than diminishing guilt in a fruitless effort to improve self-esteem, let's distinguish true guilt from neurotic or false guilt.[12] In neurotic guilt, our feeling of guilt is way out of proportion to the wrongdoing— scrupulosity. We can never quite let go of neurotic guilt, while we *can* expiate true guilt—by heading to confession!

The distinction between neurotic and real guilt is a good context for examining the proper versus improper use of psychology within Christianity. In its improper use, psychology tends to see all guilt as neurotic guilt: "Relax and become comfortable with yourself." So long as you examine your "values" and "own them," you have psychological health.

The notion of "value free" psychology was pioneered by Karl Rogers. By the end of his life, though, he recognized that there was no such thing as "value free" psychology. In trying to be value free, a person simply replaces one set of truths, say those of the Catholic tradition, with another set—those of secularity with its "faith" that truth can only be approximated if it can be known at all.

The radical fundamental option theory feeds on value free psychology, for it allows the individual freedom from mortal sin so long as he or she is still trying to love God and serve others. In this view, a true conscience does not matter; only the good (sincere) conscience is important.

In its proper use, however, psychology can be of great help dealing with difficulties that preclude the full living of the Christian life. C.S. Lewis distinguishes the moral act of choosing and the raw materials one brings to that act of choice, namely, the person's passions, emotions—the whole environmental and hereditary "package" one has. Some of those raw materials are neutral, such as the urge to defend oneself upon attack. Others are disordered, such as a kleptomaniac's urge to steal, or same-sex attraction in a homosexual person. Psychoanalysis can help repair the raw material in some instances.[13]

For instance, homosexual persons can repair their orientation, fully or to some degree.[14] There are a good number of theories about environmental causes of same-sex attraction, theories that have tested positively in clinical practice.[15] Homosexuality seems to result from fragmentations within the child/father/mother relationship, and the deepest need of the homosexual person is to repair those fragmentations. A support network called *Courage*, with groups in a variety of major cities, allows those with homosexual orientation to get help in leading a chaste life.

A person's psychological "raw material" is part of the circumstances within which moral acts are performed. And if a person commits evil but that person's "raw material" contains a proclivity toward that evil, the agent may well be less blameworthy or not blameworthy at all *(malum* without full *culpa)*.

It seems that psychology, when used properly, is an ally of Christianity. Is the same true of other "secular" disciplines?

All secular disciplines are potential allies of Christianity if they operate in a way *compatible with* the truths of the faith. That doesn't mean those disciplines must become "Christianized" in the sense of placing Christian elements, from Scripture and Tradition, all throughout. The operating principle here is called "the proper autonomy of the temporal order" (See *GS* 36 and 41, and *VS* 38.2).

Sometimes Christians are under the impression that bringing the gospel into society means "Christianizing" various aspects of it, in the sense of placing a Christian veneer over various facets of the temporal order (the Christian businessman, or the Christian spelling book for grade-school students). Or Christians might be under the impression that they ought only participate in those cultural activities that are explicitly Christian. Such mistaken impressions betray a flawed understanding of the proper autonomy of the temporal order.

Various aspects of society need not necessarily have anything explicitly Christian about them—be it entertainment, business, education, and the like. These aspects of society have their own proper autonomy, their own sets of standards. Consider some examples.

A Christian businessman might think that his operation ought to contain explicitly Christian products. Certainly there is nothing wrong with marketing Christian products, but you can be a fine businessmen without so doing. A committed Christian family might think they ought only participate in forms of entertainment explicitly Christian. Again, while there is nothing at all the matter with explicitly Christian movies, plays, or songs, entertainment can be perfectly acceptable without an explicit Christian dimension—so long as it is *compatible* with the faith.

SEVEN

THE NATURE OF THE MORAL ACT: MAKING CHRIST PRESENT IN HISTORY

When I try to insist that there are certain absolute moral prohibitions, I often get as a response, "You like to see everything in black and white." Quite a put-down. I'm accused of being a rigid "legalist" who violates Jesus' command not to judge. Any suggestions?

Keep in mind the occupational hazard of embracing participated theonomy: Someone looking at the Catholic moral life from the vantage point of autonomy will often see that life as heteronomous. They can conveniently caricature the Catholic moral life as a rigid list of heteronomous "thou shalt not's."

Try this answer, which distinguishes a heteronomous view of absolute norms from the view of participated theonomy. *Of course* the moral life is more than the bedrock of moral absolutes. But that is not to say that the moral absolutes are unimportant.

"Legalism" would hold that the moral life is reducible to following the absolute prohibitions, period. That's heteronomy! That's what the rich young man in the parable wants.

We have already visited *VS* 52, which notes that "the commandment of love of God and love of neighbor does not have in its dynamic any higher limit, but it does have a lower limit, beneath which the commandment is broken." There is no upper limit to the life of virtue—no legalism here—but the moral bedrock provides a lower limit under which we must not fall if we are to stay in right relation to God, neighbor, and self. "Furthermore, what must be done in any given situation depends on the circumstances, not all of which can be foreseen." What it means to act justly, for instance, cannot be decided in advance for each case.

VS 52 goes on to note that "on the other hand there are kinds of behavior which can never, in any situation, be a proper response—a response which is in conformity with the dignity of the person." This is the moral foundation (or "bedrock") of absolute norms. "Finally, it is always possible that man, as the result of coercion or other circumstances, can be hindered from doing certain good actions; but he can never be hindered from not doing certain actions, especially if he is prepared to die rather than to do evil."

A popular way to express this point is to say, "I'd rather die than violate a moral absolute," or "You'll make me violate the moral truth over my dead body." VS 90–93 amplifies the theme of martyrdom and its relation to moral theology.

As for being judgmental: As we noted in an earlier chapter, explain to your friend that we are not to judge someone's culpability (*culpa*)—that's God's job. But we are required to judge certain actions as incompatible with our final end (*malum*).

Recall our analogy of the river, in which you are headed toward a final destiny and must be careful not to take a wrong path incompatible with that destiny (mortal sin). When sailing on a river, all sorts of absolute rules are in the service of a safe and successful journey. These rules remind you to avoid certain practices that are incompatible with safe travel.

Following these rules insures a well-ordered trip. Violating them is a privation of due order. Only when you are "on track" can you really begin to enjoy the trip—good fishing, observing beautiful scenery and wildlife, an overall splendid trip.

In a similar way the absolute norms in the moral life are steady reminders of how to use your freedom the right way, in alignment with your ultimate destiny. To violate these norms is to lose that right alignment. Then, it is only when you are "on track" that you can do all those things that make the journey truly worthwhile—the full practice of the virtues.

In the title of this section you used the phrase "making Christ present in history." How does Christ fit into the importance of moral absolutes?

To say that we are incapable of following the bedrock of moral norms is tantamount to denying that Christ has really redeemed us. We have the grace of Christ to assist us in leading sanctified lives. And through the sacraments we not only find strength, but healing when we fail.

VS 104 notes that Christ "has set our freedom free from the domination of concupiscence." Sin entails a refusal to cooperate with the grace Christ unfailingly makes available to us. Some people say that, due to the complexities of life, no one can really be expected to follow these norms. It is right in the midst of those complexities, however, that Christ's grace shows its incredible strength.

Those who focus on the complexity of life, with an "ethics of compromise," wrong as they are about moral absolutes, are actually correct about something else: In the complexity of life, we are often hindered from doing all the good that we want to do. Consider a few examples of how external circumstances can prevent the good.

Imagine trying to contribute to your workplace—you want to improve the atmosphere. You try some extra doses of kindness, you go the extra mile for your coworkers, and the like. But it can easily happen that you get nowhere! (In fact, it can backfire on you—as the saying goes, no good deed goes unpunished.)

Or imagine trying to evangelize within your family. You are very prudent, you are not in the least pushy, but the moment any important issues come up for discussion, you are thwarted in your efforts to make a reasonable argument in favor of the Catholic faith.

Our lives are filled with instances of not accomplishing the good we would wish to accomplish. And yet we are to keep doing good, and we leave the results in God's hands.

To repeat the words of *VS* 52, which summarize these points well: "It is always possible that man, as the result of coercion or other circumstances, can be hindered from doing certain good actions; but he can never be hindered from not doing certain actions." That last point presupposes that we have been given the grace by which we can act well. The pope also notes that "there are kinds of behavior which can never, in any situation, be a proper response—a response which is in conformity with the dignity of the person." Such acts are "intrinsically evil."

And finally, the point we can't emphasize enough: The Church's firm stance on moral absolutes, and the sinfulness of violating them, must always be accompanied by the equally insistent teaching of forgiveness. Human beings can always obtain pardon and enjoy again the presence of God (see *VS* 104 and the stunning text in *CCC* 1864).

The term "intrinsic evil" is fascinating—and scary! Don't you think that plenty of people would deny that anything is intrinsically evil? "It all depends," they say.

It's important to situate intrinsic evil in the context of participated theonomy. To say that certain acts are evil in and of themselves, apart from the circumstances and intent of an agent, is to say they are contrary to the charity (sanctifying grace) dwelling within us. And since that grace is a participation in heaven, intrinsically evil acts are ones that are incompatible with our final beatific end. So when Christ, through the Church, insists that certain acts are intrinsically evil, it's not to make life hard but to help steer us toward genuine happiness.

In contrast, revisionist theologians favor some type of *proportionalist* (or *consequentialist*) method. This method essentially assumes that due to the complexities of history, the moral bedrock of absolutes exists but is far more flexible than the tradition would have us believe.[1] Proportionalists would hold that "the Church's teaching is essentially only an 'ideal' which must then be adapted, proportioned, graduated to the so-called concrete possibilities of man, according to a 'balancing of the goods in question'" (*VS* 103).

To understand proportionalism we must begin with what traditionally are called the three "fonts" or aspects of a moral act: (1) the *moral object,* or the "act itself" without any reference to the agent; (2) the *circumstances* within which an agent performs the act; and (3) the *intention* with which the agent performs the act.

1. The first font is the *moral object,* that is, the act itself—for example, the act of sterilization. This means the "raw" act or "pure" act, prior to taking into account the circumstances within which an individual, with a particular intention, might perform the act.

The debate between proportionalism and the traditional position is over whether or not there are any such acts that can be judged *intrinsically* evil, or evil in and of themselves. Otherwise put, can an act be evil by virtue of its object?

2. The second component is the *circumstances* surrounding the act. In the example of sterilization, circumstances might include the attitude of the person's spouse or family, that of the doctor, the financial situation, or the person's own health.

For proportionalism, prior to determining whether an act is right or wrong, the individual moral agent must weigh the values versus the disvalues accruing from a particular act in light of all these circumstances. As *VS* 75 describes it: "In a world where goodness is always mixed with evil, and every good effect linked to other evil effects, the morality of an act would be judged in two different ways: its moral 'goodness' would be judged on the basis of the subject's intention in reference to moral goods, and its 'rightness' on the basis of a consideration of its foreseeable effects or consequences and of their proportion."

3. The third font is actually a subcategory of the second: the *intention* of the agent, or what the agent wants to achieve by the act. For example, the agent might sterilize with any number of intentions—because the doctor said another child would be risky, because contraceptives are cumbersome, or whatever. When speaking of intention, we speak of foreseeing a future consequence, or acting in order to accomplish some desirable future consequence.

For proportionalism, we must weigh all the foreseeable consequences, or *proportion* them, in order to determine the morality of the act—hence the label "proportionalism." "Consequentialism" is an older term that has been abandoned because many other factors besides consequences are to be taken into consideration.

Sounds like the proportionalists really fail to keep the subjective aspects of the moral life distinct from the objective. But don't they claim that their system is part of the "end-oriented" or *teleological* thrust of Catholic moral theology?

VS explains that certain acts are intrinsically evil, independent of the circumstances/intentions of the agent, because they are not properly ordered (lack of *theonomy*). "Activity is morally good when it attests to and expresses the voluntary ordering of the person to his ultimate end and the conformity of a concrete action with the human good as it is acknowledged in its truth by reason" (72, also see 78–79).

For example, sexual intercourse is morally good when it is ordered to (an expression of) permanent commitment, and when it is thus ordered, it is simultaneously ordered to our *ultimate* end. So actions *are* in fact determined to be good by their consequences.

But the determinative consequences are *not the consequences as subjectively perceived* by the agent, as the proportionalists see it. Rather, the determinative consequences are the *objective* consequences that are *intrinsic* to an act. Sex has right within it the objective consequence of expressing permanent commitment, and the ultimate consequence of the agent arriving at his or her final end.

To act in such a way that denies those *intrinsic* consequences (Thomas calls them *per se* consequences) is therefore *intrinsically* disordered (evil). Such objective, intrinsic consequences are separate from the perceived subjective consequences of an agent (such as "Sex will relieve my partner's loneliness, it will make us feel good, it will solidify our friendship"). Study *VS* 74 and 75 here.

The Thomistic tradition has *just* the term to capture the idea that actions, to be moral, must be properly ordered *toward* their right ends and toward the ultimate end: It speaks of the action as the "end of the act," the *finis operis* (as distinct from the "ends of the agent," the *fines operantis*). Properly understood, then, the Catholic moral tradition is heavily "end oriented" or *teleological.*

You can almost feel the *dynamism* of this perspective: We really are *headed somewhere* in our moral lives. We're headed toward the good life, which has its ultimate crown in the beatific vision.

That's the way God planned or ordered it. Why not enjoy it? Why not *participate* in God's marvelous order (*theonomy*)?

VS 80 includes a list of actions that are intrinsically evil, taken from *GS* 27, and the examples include genocide, abortion, euthanasia, arbitrary imprisonment, deportation, slavery, prostitution, and degrading conditions of work. The Ten Commandments provide a kind of organizational framework within which we can categorize every area of the moral life, such as social matters, matters of marriage and family, sexual ethics, and bioethics. *CCC* 2052–2557—an enormous section—lays out all of this.

I love the distinction between *malum* and *culpa*. Can you give a succinct re-cap of the church's position, and then proportionalism, using those terms?

You bet—and here are three points which, if mastered, allow a perfect grasp of the Church's position on intrinsic evil in contrast to the proportionalist mistake—call these the "master points."

1. Good intent and difficult circumstances cannot make an intrinsically evil act—a *malum*—into a good act (*VS* 81). A good end does not justify a *malum* (the thief who plans to donate much, or all, of his money, does not suddenly act virtuously).

2. However, good intent and difficult circumstances might make a person less blameworthy for a particular act (*VS* 62, 70, 77, and 104). (Consider the woman having an abortion under tremendous pressure from family and boyfriend.)

3. Finally—and here's a new point—intention and other circumstances can affect a good or neutral act in several ways. They can turn a neutral or good act into something less than good. (A person might pray so as to impress someone, or give a donation to charity to enhance his prestige.) Or intention and circumstance can make a good act even more praiseworthy (helping someone when you have a headache, for example). Let's also introduce a diagram at this point, showing the three fonts of the moral act.

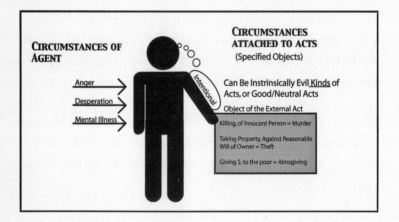

Got it. Now, on to proportionalism.

Proportionalists claim that no acts *in themselves* are morally evil (*malum*). Acts can only be described as morally evil when intention and circumstances come into play. Until then they are called *pre-moral* evils.

For example, some argue that homosexual activity is a pre-moral evil—it is not an ideal phenomenon, but it is not morally good or evil until the agent's intentions are added. If it is engaged in for pure sensual delight, it could be morally evil, but if there is commitment and friendship, then the intention is good and there is no moral evil.

Or consider again sterilization. Proportionalists would say that by itself it is pre-morally evil, which is to say that it is not in and of itself the kind of activity we would seek after. But it is not intrinsically evil.

If there is a proportionate reason, they would argue, sterilization may be a morally good act. That is to say, if the agent has carefully weighed the values and disvalues that might accrue from the act, and if the values outweigh the disvalues, the act is moral. Put technically, pre-moral evils are morally justifiable if there is a proportionate reason. "In this view, deliberate consent to certain kinds of behavior declared illicit by traditional moral theology would not imply an objective moral evil" (*VS* 75).

"Pre-moral" evil is a term that the Catholic moral tradition rejects. But another term is of importance in the debate—material evil—and this term is very important in the Catholic moral tradition. An example of material evil would be amputation of a limb.

The key point about "mere" material evil is that it has no *moral* connotations all by itself. It *could* be morally evil; consider the doctor who does some operation that is really unnecessary just to collect insurance money. But in many cases to cause a material evil is entirely moral, and is justified by what the tradition has termed the "principle of totality."

According to this principle, we can commit material evil if it is for the good of the whole organism. So if someone were to die unless a limb were amputated, the amputation would be justified by the principle of totality. On the other hand, amputations performed by Nazi doctors for purposes of medical experimentation would be morally evil.

Here's a great little test. Look at those last two sentences. Do they look just a little like proportionalism? If you said yes, you'll see why proportionalists themselves confuse material evil with so called "pre-moral evil."

Now part II of the test: What's the difference? There is no question that a material evil bears surface similarity with "pre-moral" evil in the sense that it is an action that exists prior to a moral evaluation, and it is morally neutral prior to being placed in a moral context. If you saw a silent film of an amputation, or of a gunshot wound, you would be seeing material evil but would not be able to assign any moral evaluation.

Proportionalists, however, include a much wider range of activity under the rubric "pre-moral" evil. All the activity that the tradition would call intrinsically evil is labeled pre-moral evil. If you saw a silent film showing an act of euthanasia, you would be seeing a material evil that is also intrinsically evil. For the proportionalist, you would be seeing a pre-moral evil, since an act of euthanasia might be justifiable if the values outweighed the disvalues.

I'm a bit dumbfounded. I can see secularists teaching this, but how can proportionalists possibly claim to be Catholic?

Believe it or not, the proportionalists actually argue that they are very much in continuity with the Tradition. They claim that when the Tradition speaks of intrinsically evil acts, in many cases it has already added a circumstance or intention to a material act—and only after that can the acts be said to be intrinsically evil. For instance:

1. The Tradition never claims that killing is evil. Rather, killing in some circumstances is evil. In other circumstances it is legitimate. Killing an innocent person is evil, but killing an unjust aggressor is morally licit.

2. The Tradition never claims that taking property is evil. Rather, taking property *in some circumstances* is evil, and in other circumstances it is legitimate—if it is not against the reasonable will of the owner.

3. The Tradition never claims that telling a falsehood is evil. Rather, telling a falsehood to someone who has a right to know the truth is evil and is a lie.

Having noted such examples, proportionalists then go on to make an interesting accusation against the Tradition. Many so-called intrinsically evil acts already have circumstance and intention included within them (murder, lying, stealing). But other so-called intrinsically evil acts do not, and are said to be evil by virtue of the moral object itself (sterilization, contraception, homosexual acts).

In this light, they demand consistency of the Catholic Tradition. Since all intrinsically evil acts are really material acts further delineated by circumstance and intention, why not allow circumstance and intention to affect the evil of an act in *every case?*

For instance, if killing is evil only under certain circumstances, then why is sterilization always evil in and of itself? Why not say that sterilization, like killing, is pre-morally evil, or materially evil, but can become a morally good activity under certain circumstances?

I'm afraid to admit this, but that sounds—don't tell anyone—somewhat convincing. What gives?

When I explain this material to students in the classroom, I give them a couple minutes' break right at this point. Then I tell them they have a new advantage in their next discussion with someone veering toward proportionalism and relativism. They can honestly say, "You know, I once entertained proportionalism myself, but I found it intellectually vacuous, and morally it was a real dead-end."

But back to work! It is true that when the Tradition labels something as intrinsically evil, it does so by specifying a moral object with certain circumstances. This is certainly the case in the examples given above regarding murder, theft, and lying. But these circumstances have nothing to do with *a particular agent* and the particular consequences of that agent's act.

It is crucial not to confuse such circumstances, which help describe the moral object, with the other two fonts of the moral act, namely the circumstances and intention *of the agent.* In fact, it's a good idea to call them *specifications* and leave the word *circumstances* on the side of the particular agent. With this distinction, we can speak of the three fonts in a fresh light.

A moral object that is intrinsically evil will always bear some specifications. Murder is killing *of the innocent*. Lying is a false-hood *to one who has the right to know the truth*. You can fill in a new feature in our diagram above—the moral object is always a *specified* object.

Then, the circumstances/intentions/consequences on the side of the agent performing such acts can be kept separate from the moral object. They won't make the intrinsically evil act into a good act. But they may affect the culpability of the agent (there are the first two "master points" again).

For example, the killing of an innocent person (the specified moral object) can be done by someone in dire circumstances or by a person with a noble intent. Someone who is in dire poverty might abort a child with the intent of helping her existing family survive. These actions still fall under the category *malum*, but the culpability would certainly be less than if they had been done for purely selfish reasons.

When we look to the arena of sexual conduct, the same type of analysis applies. For example, the nature of the conjugal act as unitive and procreative should never be violated (recall chapter 4). Here the conjugal act is *specified* in a particular way that clearly rules out anti-procreative contraception and sterilization.

If someone contracepts, that person engages in a moral act that is intrinsically evil. The circumstances and the intention of the agent are kept separate from the object. Someone might contracept in dire circumstances (a demanding spouse) with good intentions (to keep a marriage together), which may affect culpability, but not the intrinsic evil of the act itself.

In light of this example, we can critique Richard McCormick's request to describe "sterilization *against the good of the marriage*" as the object. Such sterilization is already by definition (or by specification) against the good of marriage.

You have probably noticed that for proportionalism the specifying of the moral object is ultimately left up to the individual. That's a pretty big burden to place on a person. For the Catholic moral tradition, no one person has the burden of arbitrating over what's right and what's wrong. The Holy Spirit, guiding Tradition and Scripture, and guiding the apostolic succession in the proper interpretation of these, has clearly told the Christian community, through its history, that there are some acts that in themselves are incompatible with charity, acts that are intrinsically evil.

Now a bit of good news. Since the promulgation of *Veritatis Splendor* in 1993, there seems to have been a steady decline in academic attention given to proportionalism. While on the practical level it's as alive as ever, we can look forward to fewer and fewer students and seminarians being handed this theory under the guise of Catholic moral teaching. But we still must be alert and vigilant. A lot of people have been damaged by this misleading theory, especially when it got out of the scholarly journals and into pastoral practice—into our schools and parishes.

Well, along those lines, can you show exactly how it works in practice? It sounds to me as if people who learn this theory could easily buy into relativism, with adverse impact on their lives.

Imagine students studying the topic of moral norms in their course on moral theology. They come in knowing that the moral norms of the Church have an absolute character to them—the Ten Commandments are not The Ten Suggestions. And in fact their professor affirms these moral norms, but as a proportionalist affirms them—as *ideals*. He notes that everyone should always strive to follow them—as ideals they are not negotiable.

However, because of the sheer complexity of life, the professor insists, there are rare situations in which one may justifiably fall short of a particular high ideal, due to exceptionally difficult circumstances and sincere intentions. Some proportionalist teachers would come right out and say such situations are not rare at all.

The proportionalist professor's motive is pastoral compassion for those in truly challenging situations. But there's the rub: The very nature of our moral lives is that we find ourselves in challenging moral quandaries, situations in which we come up against a solid moral norm and wonder, *Might my case be the rare exception to this absolute principle?* Or put a bit less academically: *There's a rule out there but I might have to break it.*

That is a prime instance of the concupiscent tendency at work. When the professor presents a system that allows rare exceptions, he places the students on a dangerous trajectory. They will soon conclude that they themselves constitute the rare exception. A theory that academically allows rare exceptions, when put into practice, justifies a multitude of exceptions.

Ironically, a theory that wants to add a dose of compassion to people's lives turns out not to be compassionate at all.

Rather, the method places an undue burden on people—
ultimately the burden of trying to be God. As human agents
we are incapable of the kind of weighing required by proportionalist methodology.

We can easily assess what we think we want for ourselves.
But we are often blinded to what our deepest needs are.
Concupiscence gets in the way. Not taking full cognizance of
this fact is perhaps the deepest flaw in proportionalist method.

Even apart from the wound of concupiscence in the will,
our intellects are simply incapable of the kind of calculation
required by proportionalism. *VS* makes precisely this point:

> Moreover, everyone recognizes the difficulty, or rather
> the impossibility, of evaluating all the good and evil con-
> sequences and effects—defined as pre-moral—of one's
> own acts: an exhaustive rational calculation is not pos-
> sible. How then can one go about establishing propor-
> tions which depend on a measuring, the criteria of which
> remain obscure? How could an absolute obligation be
> justified on the basis of such debatable calculations? (78)

The best that proportionalism can do for a person, it would
seem, is give a good estimate of what might be a moral or
immoral act. While at first sight this may look like humility in
the face of human complexity, it is finally unfair to the human
agent to have the burden of living in so vague a moral world.
Many of our daily moral decisions, including nearly all decisions regarding our sexuality, involve perfectly clear-cut
answers.

Of course—here are the "master points" again—the complex

circumstances surrounding an act, while not affecting the wrongness of the act, may well affect the culpability of the agent. Yet this is not for us to decide, but for God. The right thing to do remains clear, and for us to deny this is to make ourselves arbiters over the moral life, to be as gods.

Individuals may have a clouded vision of the right thing to do, which would be all the more reason to have a Church that can clearly and consistently proclaim the moral truth we are asked to live out in history. Once a person is oriented to his proper end (which ultimately is God, but proximately includes the moral requirements of Catholic life), he can become a saint. But that orientation is not easy—the Catholic community is a necessity. Without that community, or without that community speaking with a unified voice, disorientation is inevitable.

It is customary among revisionists to dichotomize an "ethics of act" and an "ethics of virtue or character." It is argued that in a complex world, in which the morality of specific acts remains clouded with ambiguity, it is better to focus on "the kind of person we ought to become." But for participated theonomy the two types of ethical analysis are both integral to the Catholic understanding of the moral life.

There exists a certain bedrock of moral norms (an ethics of act) upon which we can build our moral life. Given this, we do not have the overwhelming burden of having to arbitrate over moral truth each step of the way. We ought not abort, cheat, contracept, and so on.

But it is obviously no easy task, given the complexities of life, to live out the moral truth we are given. Only with a life of virtue can this be done. So the couple who wishes to contracept or abort, or the businessman who would find it most convenient to cheat, need do no proportional weighing as Catholics. They simply don't abort, contracept, cheat, or what have you.

Admittedly, the challenge of living out such decisions demands much virtue as we confront obstacles at each step of the way. The life of virtue is inexhaustive, but at bottom it involves the living out of those moral norms which provide a moral bedrock, immune from any calculus, for the moral agent.

Read *VS:* 71–83.
Study *CCC:* 1749–56.

Proportionalism sure is dangerous! I've heard it claimed by proportionalists that St. Thomas himself would be sympathetic to their theory, and that Thomas in fact comes right out and says that "actions are right or wrong according to their circumstances." Is that true?

While Thomas does state that (q. 18, a. 3), it is in that part of an article (the objections and the *sed contra*) that is posing the various positions held by others, which Thomas then goes on to answer and clarify. But you've cut me to the quick: Fasten your seat belts, because we cannot resist the opportunity to learn more about the moral act from St. Thomas.

Thomas says that in an act, there is a twofold activity taking place: the external act itself, and the interior act of the will. Consider a person giving alms during the Sunday collection.

The external act of placing a twenty into the basket has an object, and the object is almsgiving. This is a specific instance of a certain kind of act, an "almsgiving-kind-of-act." That is an intrinsically good act, one that is highly compatible with the agent's ultimate beatific end.

We could break this object down even more, noting that the object in the most raw, material sense is giving money, and that a specifying circumstance enters the object, namely giving money *that will go to the poor.* That specifying circumstance is what makes this act of giving money into an act called almsgiving. And it is the ordered nature of almsgiving—its objectively good end or consequences—that makes it a good kind of act (a good *finis operis* or "end of the act").

Now let's look inside the agent—and here we complete the diagram begun earlier. It would be nice to make the assumption that the agent is highly virtuous, and that what he intends is nothing other than generous almsgiving ordered toward helping the poor. A twenty is a lot for this person, but he easily gives it, knowing the dire need of the poor to whom the money will go.

What is happening inside the agent's mind (the ends of the agent, or *fines operantis*), in relation to the external object? This interior act *has its object*, and in this case the object of the interior will matches the object of the external act—the agent intends the act of almsgiving to aid the poor. In this happy case, both objects are good. In the expanded diagram, see the two "boxes."

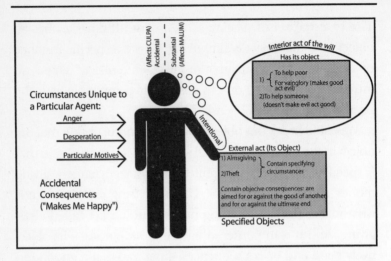

Now change the scenario so that the object of the external act remains identical, but the object of the interior act of the will is drastically different. The individual would normally give a token pittance, maybe a dollar. But in this instance, he knows that his boss is sitting behind him, in a position to see easily what he is preparing to put in the basket.

Wanting to impress his boss (the possibility of a raise looms), he pulls a twenty out of his wallet and holds it in a rather conspicuous position while waiting for the basket to arrive. The object of the interior act of the will would be called vainglory. (In most such cases, that object would in fact be mixed, and we are left wondering whether the agent is more a seeker of vainglory or more an almsgiver.)

The object of the interior act is technically called the "end." This is at first confusing, because the three fonts of the moral act are object, intent (read "the end I seek"), and circumstances, and it seems we have just "blended" object and intent (end). But in point of fact, the term "object" is broader than normally thought, and covers both the object of the external act and the object of the interior act of the will.

One more point: The man who is almsgiving for vainglory still is deliberately performing an "almsgiving-kind-of-act." In our diagram, that deliberate choice is indicated at the man's hand. But it could just as well be pictured up inside the agent's intent, not as his ultimate end (vainglory) but as his proximate end (putting a twenty in the basket, a twenty that will in fact help the poor).

How are you doing so far? Check the footnote if you want to hear this straight from the master himself.[2]

The second font, intent, is also broader than commonly thought. As just noted, it covers the interior act of the will that has its object. But it also covers something else. Notice that in the above two scenarios, we spoke abstractly about "an agent." The acts described could apply to any number of different agents. We didn't consider the various things going on inside *a particular agent*, namely, the circumstances and intent *on the side of the particular agent*, for assessing a *particular* act is different from assessing a *kind* of act.

For instance, name the agent "Joe," and imagine that Joe has just found out that his daughter's medical bills will soon be astronomical—hence, the circumstances of this particular agent (as opposed to objective circumstances that specify an object). He is still seeking something for himself more than for the poor in his act of giving twenty dollars. But his desire for a raise has nothing to do with the new boat he longs for and everything to do with the well-being of his family—so we have the intent of this particular agent, or what might better be termed Joe's *motive*.

Recall that these circumstances and intentions *on the side of the agent* cannot make an evil act good, but they can greatly affect the culpability, or lack thereof, that the agent will bear.

Now shift the case: Joe engages in an act of theft in order to pay his daughter's bills. The external object—taking property against the reasonable will of the owner—is intrinsically evil (note that it is a specified object). The object of the interior act of the will is good—aiding someone in need—but will not turn an intrinsically evil act into a good act. It will affect culpability, as will the particular circumstances: The particular person in need, the daughter, is in great pain.

In sum, the three fonts of the moral act each have dual meanings:

1. The *object* can refer to (a) the object of the external act, or (b) the object of the interior act, also called the "end."

2. *Intent* can refer to (a) the end just mentioned, also called the object of the interior act of the will, which can be outlined without reference to any particular agent, or (b) the motive of the particular agent.

3. *Circumstances* can refer to (a) those objective circumstances or specifications which can enter the object of the external act and which can be outlined without any reference to a particular agent, or (b) the unique circumstances of a particular agent.

I can't believe I'm thinking through all of this at so high a level—it's not as hard as I thought, and it sure is helpful. Can we try a couple more examples now? What about a thief who carefully plans a robbery, but due to illness, or because his partner doesn't show up, never follows through? Has he sinned?

Or to re-phrase your question—participated theonomy here: Is there a moral object he has engaged in that is incompatible with his ultimate end? If a policeman suspects him, he can easily note that he has done nothing, and in the eyes of the civil law he's guiltless. But in the eyes of the natural, divine, and eternal law he is guilty, due to the object of the interior act of the will.

The fact that he never got around to the external act is a happy fact for society. But he has materially sinned (though the sin is less grave for not having an external object). Then, his circumstances and especially his motives may well affect his culpability (formal sin). While he might be out for pure personal gain, perhaps he lives in a very unjust social setting and is robbing a bakery in order to provide food for his family.

Keep in mind that at a certain point, circumstances could enter—or specify—the object, making it something other than theft. Recall that theft is taking property against the reasonable will of the owner. Perhaps the baker has refused to give the man bread that will be thrown out anyway, and there is no other way for the man reasonably to obtain food. At that point, the man no longer commits theft.

This philosophic analysis explains Christ's challenge regarding the virtue of purity: that a man who looks lustfully at a woman commits adultery. The sinful object is in the interior act of the will. Should the man actually carry out adultery as an external object, the gravity of his sin would be weightier.[3] Again, his own circumstances and motives affect his culpability. (For instance, he may have been seduced by someone who convinced him that this act would be a compassionate way to relieve her loneliness.)

Could there be a case in which an individual commits an evil external act, and the interior act of the will is completely good?

This actually happens quite often, so I'm glad you mentioned it! Whenever there is complete invincible ignorance (go way back to chapter 1) this would be the simple case of the false and good conscience. Imagine a girl having an abortion, but under the illusion that she is just having some tissue removed. She's been totally duped by Planned Parenthood and has never heard a good pro-life presentation showing what the fetus really is—a human being, not an object.

As to her subjective motive, let's say that her mother is pressuring her to have the abortion, and she sincerely wants to please her mother. When she has the abortion, she engages in the kind of act that, in and of itself, is intrinsically evil. But if you asked her, "What are you doing?" her honest response would be, "I am having tissue removed."

That's the object of her interior act of the will. There is no formal sin involved. Material sin, yes (*Malum,* yes. *Culpa,* no.)

Now let's add the following scenario: Between the time of

her initial decision and the actual abortion, she hears a good (non-heteronomous) pro-life presentation at her high school. Suddenly she realizes that her interior act of the will is mistaken.

Education has assisted her in getting the interior act of the will to *match* the external act—that's a nice description of what happens when we convince someone not to do something that's wrong. For the girl, what previously was an upcoming material sin now is an upcoming formal sin. If she proceeds with the abortion, she is sinning, though her culpability may be mitigated given the continued pressure from her mother.

In both cases, we have been assuming that the girl was about to *choose freely*, or *will*, the act of abortion. Without such choice[4] there could be no sin (recall the three conditions for sin). Now imagine her mother (who knows perfectly well what a fetus is) pressuring her to have the abortion. At this point, the girl does an intrinsically evil kind of act (the object of the external act), and she knows very well what she is doing (the object of the interior act of the will, or the end), but because of the *pressure* (as opposed to the earlier lack of knowledge) the girl's culpability is lessened.

Now travel quickly to China. There, a woman is literally *forced* by the authorities to have an abortion. Due to the coercion there is no sin. The authorities in this case are the ones sinning.

I think I'm putting it all together—all the components of the "whole moral act." I never thought it would be this much fun to "think with St. Thomas." But now I need practice. Can you

provide some more examples on which I could try out each component in the master diagram?

For that, you'll have to turn to the web site! You'll find plenty of examples and exercises there, and if you get stuck you can email yours truly. See you in cyberspace!

Here's what I like about the Catholic moral life: While the moral life may be challenging, we need not be conflicted when it comes to discovering the applicable moral norm. There is an authority outside of ourselves.

But what about those rare cases in which it really is difficult to figure out what to do? I'm thinking of the really tough "heartbreak" cases, such as when a woman has to choose between her own life and her unborn child's life.

There are certain cases—Thomas says "some few cases" (94, 4)—that are "conflict situations." In these cases, few and far between, the absolute norm is applicable in a rather complicated way. Proportionalists think this constitutes an "exception" and then wish to argue that all cases are somewhat like this, admitting of exceptions, at least in principle.

In these rare complicated cases, we need a wise person not only capable of all the pertinent philosophical distinctions, but also able to apply those distinctions to particular cases. Here we can outline some of those distinctions that traditionally have been used in Catholic moral theology, along with generic examples.

Actually, we have already had occasion to examine one such set of distinctions. Recall that specifying circumstances can actually change the moral object, making it good instead of evil or evil instead of good. Recall that the moral object is always a specified object—that is, it is a material object with a specifying circumstance or intent that places it in a moral category.

For example, "One should never kill an innocent person" is a specified prohibition against killing. Should a new specifying circumstance—an unjust aggressor—render it just to kill, then a new circumstance has changed the object and the person killing is doing nothing morally evil at all.

Or, regarding property, Thomas says you should always return property to the rightful owner (stated negatively, never steal). But what if a person whose gun you have asks for it back, and you know he is going to use it against the common good (see q. 94, a. 4)? Here a new specifying circumstance changes the moral object. Your not giving him the gun is not an act of theft or a failure to return property.

Earlier we talked about the "principle of totality." Would that fit here? Can we review it?

Right. The principle of totality is most often invoked in medical situations when a part of the body must intentionally be mutilated—something as serious as amputation or as commonplace as pulling a tooth. The one part can be sacrificed for the sake of the health of the whole body. This is allowable because each bodily organ is not an end in itself, but exists for the sake of the whole body. Since it is not an end in itself, its removal does not constitute a moral evil, but only a physical evil.

The principle is often misused in religious discussion groups or classes in which the ulterior motive is to pave the way for some brand of situational ethics (which tries to justify a *moral* evil for the sake of some larger good). Students are asked whether they would kill an individual if by so doing they could save a large number of people. Some try to justify the killing in light of the principle of totality, forgetting that each human life is an end in itself, and that therefore intentional killing constitutes a moral evil.

Another misuse of the principle is outlined in the encyclical *Humanae Vitae:*

> By extending to this field the application of the so-called "principle of totality," could it not be admitted that the intention of a less abundant but more rationalized fecundity might transform a materially sterilizing intervention into a licit and wise control of birth? Could it not be admitted, that is, that the finality of procreation pertains to the ensemble of conjugal life, rather than to its single acts? (3)

Put simply, can't a couple contracept, recognizing that the procreative dimension of certain conjugal acts is sacrificed for the sake of the whole marriage, so long as a procreative dimension exists somewhere during the marriage?

This would only be licit, however, if the conjugal act did not have its own inherent dignity—if it only existed for the sake of the whole marriage. In fact, although each act does exist for the sake of the whole marriage, each act also has its own inherent dignity (as Paul VI goes on to show in the encyclical). The conjugal act is not analogous to a bodily organ that exists only for the health of the whole body. Hence, the principle of totality does not apply.

I was recently in a situation where I literally couldn't escape doing evil—lucky for me, the evil I chose was minuscule. To prevent a shelf from tipping and harming my daughter, I had to step on—and break—the very nice but delicate art project of my son. No moral evil, I hope!

We must choose the lesser of the two evils in such a situation, and then that lesser evil is not a moral evil but only a material evil—no *culpa*. A less minuscule example that I hope you never encounter: A driver is forced off the highway right near a roadside picnic area, and in swerving to avoid ten picnickers, that driver will invariably hit two others. Obviously, the principle applies here, and the driver reluctantly chooses the lesser of two evils.

Another possible example is one given in the novel *Sophie's Choice*. Sophie has two children, and in the death camp where normally both would be killed, she is allowed to keep one (because of the Germans' admiration for her father). She must choose.

Some moralists would say that she can use the principle of the lesser of two evils and make the dreadful choice, thereby at least preventing the death of one child. Others reject such reasoning, noting that the mother is being made a victim of a moral blackmail in which she should simply not take part. She ought not arbitrate over life, and she must tell the guards that they ought not either. This puts the burden of killing not on her but on those blackmailing her.

That fictional case might be illuminated by the following historical one, in which a German city-dweller during the Nazi regime is discovered on a bridge giving some small assistance to a Jewish street urchin. The guard tells him to throw the boy into the water to his death, or else both he and the boy will be shot. While the man did as he was told, he later committed suicide over this, a result which, while highly tragic, tells us that the principle of the lesser of two evils was inapplicable here. Another option, heroic as it was, was available.

There are many instances like this in which the principle would seem to apply but finally does not, since the individual need not choose either of the evils involved. The recent controversy over prevention of AIDS is such an instance. On the one hand, there is the evil of sexual activity outside of a monogamous relationship. Even worse, it is argued, is the evil of such activity when it is "unprotected," since disease may result.

For this reason, some suggest that the Church ought to promote educational efforts about AIDS prevention, and that such involvement would be justified by the principle of the lesser of two evils. However, the Church need not have anything to do with promoting either of the evils involved, and so the principle simply does not apply in this case. She ought only to teach constantly the truths necessary to avoid such evils in the first place (truths about chastity), and promote the corporal works of mercy among the faithful toward all those who have the disease.[1]

Finally, we might note that this principle is the basis upon which we could justify the buildup of a nuclear arsenal for deterrent purposes. There is intent to use if necessary, thereby endangering civilians and causing destruction on a massive scale. The other, greater, evil is the loss of liberty.

So, it is argued, we can reasonably echo the slogan "Give me liberty or give me death," based on the lesser-of-two-evils principle. Of course, a nation would be obligated to do everything in its power to negotiate a mutual reduction of arms.

Our family recently had a tough decision regarding a terminally ill relative. For her comfort, we had to increase the amount of painkiller considerably. The morphine ended up quickening her death. Some family members felt some guilt about that, but they didn't want to see her in so much pain.

No guilt required! In a fallen world, there are times when an action causes both a good and an evil effect. A similar example: withholding treatment from a terminally ill patient, thus hastening the impending death. The "Principle of Double Effect" (PDE) governs such cases (see *CCC* 1737, 2263).

To discover when it is legitimate to perform such acts, which produce both a good and an evil effect, four criteria must be met:

1. *The moral object must be good or neutral, not intrinsically evil.* The PDE presupposes, contrary to proportionalism, that there are such things as intrinsically evil acts. In the example, the acts of withholding treatment or providing pain medication are not intrinsically evil.

2. *The evil result is tolerated, not intended; the good effect is what the agent intends.* Then, the evil effect stems *indirectly* from the act, while the good effect stems *directly* from it. The PDE presupposes that there is a morally significant difference between

direct and indirect actions (whereas proportionalism mistakenly sees the difference as accidental). The death is not intended, but tolerated; the intent is to respect nature/God's will and to relieve pain.

3. *The good effect doesn't occur as a result of the evil effect* (you can't do evil to achieve good). In the example, the relief of pain does not come about as a result of the death, but just the reverse.

4. *There must be a proportionate reason for doing the act; included among these reasons must be the unavailability of other alternatives.* Note that the act of "proportionate reasoning" here is not the same as proportional*ism*. There are numerous situations in life that call for such weighing; what is prohibited is to use proportionate reasoning in an attempt to justify an intrinsically evil act.

If the particular case passes through these four conditions "unsnagged," then the agent only indirectly causes the evil, and hence the act is moral.

How about some more examples using PDE—some that pass the criteria, and some that get "snagged" on one or another of them?

In the famous Karen Anne Quinlan case, the parents argued that Karen, who was in a coma, be removed from the respirator. Previously, attempts to wean her from the respirator had not worked, and so there was a good chance that she would die should the treatment be removed. Here, the good effect is the placing of a life into "nature's" or God's hands, so to speak. The extraordinary means of keeping the person breathing are burdensome and may well be preventing the person's natural time of death. The bad effect is the death itself.

This case passes through all four criteria. The act of removing extraordinary treatment is neutral. The parents intend the good effect and tolerate or allow the death. The death is not caused by the removal of treatment, but by the body's natural inability to breathe. And finally, given the burdensomeness of "forcing" life onto someone whose time to die has come, the means are proportionate.

Surprisingly, when the respirator was removed Karen started to breathe on her own. Had the intent been to kill her, the logical thing to do would have been to take further steps, such as removing the IV. Had the parents secretly wished they could have done this, or even have had a lethal injection administered, then their intent *would have been* to kill, and the act of removing the respirator would have been wrong—a prime example of how intent can make an otherwise good or neutral act into an evil act.

In actuality, the parents cared for her in a comatose state for a number of years, until she died of natural causes. This case "proved" the validity of the principle, especially the second point: the moral distinction between direct and indirect.

Some other proper uses of PDE include the following. When a doctor treats a patient with a contagious disease, he risks catching the disease himself. This is not intended, but tolerated. The same is true of the policeman who risks his life to capture a criminal.

In the case of shipwreck survivors oft-used in the classroom, men dive off a raft, swimming as long as they are able, so that those remaining will have enough food to last until possible rescue. They do not head for certain death, as a rescue plane might arrive any time. Should they die, their deaths are tolerated, not intended. No one killed them, nor did they commit suicide.

Cases that get snagged on one or another of the criteria include the sheriff who frames a man to calm a raging mob. Here the act itself is evil since the innocent man is directly and intentionally killed, and the good comes as a direct result of the bad effect.

Or consider the "carpet bombing" of World War II, in which pilots dropped bombs indiscriminately on a city as a scare tactic. Some tried to justify it, claiming that the act itself was neutral—dropping a bomb—and that they were only "allowing" innocent civilians to die. In fact, the act itself is the killing of innocent people. Their deaths are intended, and the good effect comes about directly as a result of the evil effect.

Finally, consider the druggist selling poisons to a person whom he knows will use them indiscriminately. The druggist cannot say that he is "allowing" the evil of indiscriminate use to occur. Here, the circumstance enters into the act itself, and the druggist is guilty by association of the indiscriminate use— say, the suicide.

This is an important principle for business ethics. A case in point: We cannot sell pornography and claim that the resulting evil is merely allowed rather than intended.

How about further clarifying the difference between the removal of treatment from terminally ill patients and euthanasia? Many who pushed for Oregon's assisted suicide law claimed the two are essentially the same—and since we already do the former, let's allow the latter as well.

Those favoring assisted suicide argued, as good proportionalists, that the direct/indirect distinction is only an accidental distinction. As William E. May has insightfully noted, the proportionalists may have confused the direct/indirect distinction with another distinction, that of omission/commission.[2]

In the latter, we are aware that sin can be committed by both committing an act and by failing to act. There is no substantial difference between the two, only an accidental difference. An example would be active and passive euthanasia. If I kill an elderly patient, or a newborn with a birth defect, by simply ignoring him for a week, I in essence have done the same thing as if I were to kill him with a gun or lethal injection. Or to take another example, if I ignore the needs of the poor around me, I do the same essential act as if I were intentionally to harm a poverty-stricken person.

The direct/indirect distinction is of a different kind, and there is a substantial difference between directly intending an act and indirectly allowing an act. When I stop using extraordinary means on a terminally ill person, there is a remote sense in which my act kills him—my act is *connected* to his death. Yet we would never say that I directly killed him.

My direct act was removing or withholding disproportionate treatment so as to respect his dignity and allow life to take its natural course. I do not will his death; rather, I allow it. The same kind of analysis could be fairly applied to a variety of other examples that "pass" the PDE.

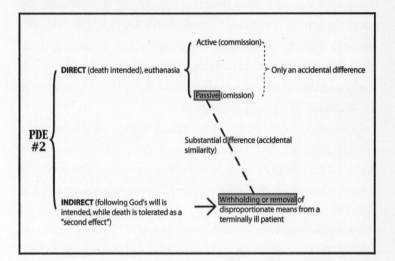

In sum, the proportionalists often confuse the commission/omission distinction, in which the difference is but accidental, with the direct/indirect distinction, in which the difference is substantial. They conclude that the direct/indirect distinction—an essential component of the traditional PDE—should be abandoned. That's the error behind legalized euthanasia, whether in the Netherlands or in Oregon.

My friend got a summer job at a video store to help pay for college. Unfortunately, he found out that the store carried some soft-core porn. It would have been hard to find another job, and certainly one that paid decently. What should he have done?

Perhaps one of the most useful distinctions comes to the fore here—material versus formal cooperation with evil. There are many times in our lives when we realize that alongside the good we try to do—your friend works hard at the summer job—we find ourselves complicit in some evil. Assuming there is no simple alternative (an equally good job down the street that's squeaky clean), what should we do? How do we inform the conscience in such situations?

Let's use an easy example to get us started. Robbers come out of a bank as you are parking nearby and force you to drive them to the airport in their getaway car. You give material cooperation, not formal. (In fact, you go straight to the police!)

Compare this with volunteering to take a friend to an abortion clinic. You align your intent with her intent—exactly what we mean by formal cooperation.

In sixteenth-century London, medical students wanted to dissect corpses, which was strictly forbidden. Rampant street crime provided a source of corpses, and students used them. Were they formal cooperators of the murderers? No, because they did not share the murderers' intentions.

Although material cooperation is licit, there's an important rule of thumb to follow: We must keep our material cooperation with evil as remote as possible. If the robbers force *you* to rob the bank, that's no longer so remote. If the terrorists force the pilot to steer the plane into the building, that's not very remote either.

At a certain point the material cooperation is not at all remote, but very proximate or immediate: A nurse, against abortion herself, hands the abortionist his tools. At that point, the material cooperation is illicit. The less remote the cooperation, the more we should be seeking alternatives. As in each of the principles for conflict situations, the individual conscience has a unique role to play.

Often when you play your part in the political process—voting—the question of cooperation with evil arises. Can you vote for a candidate whose platform allows for abortion in cases of rape and incest, but who is otherwise a desirable, if imperfect, candidate? What if there is another candidate, with a more pure position, who nonetheless does not stand a realistic chance of election? You may vote for the first candidate, materially cooperating with that part of his platform which falls short of the ideal.[3]

Of the various principles for dealing with the tough cases, which one would be used for dealing with the question of just war?

The principle of double effect (PDE) is the one. Not only does PDE fit perfectly here, it was originally developed by St. Thomas (II-II, q. 64, a. 7) precisely to explain why it is morally licit to harm an unjust aggressor—one part of the "just war doctrine" that had been fleshed out throughout the tradition, with special impetus from St. Augustine.

We divide just war doctrine into three parts. The first two sets of criteria fall under the heading *Ius ad bellum* ("right *to* war"), indicating that the criteria will tell us (a) under what conditions it is right to resort to warfare, and (b) whether it would be prudent to do what we might have a right to do. The third set falls under the heading *Ius in bello* (right *in* war), under which we will find criteria about what is right to do once we are in the midst of warfare.

So first, the criteria for *Ius ad bellum:*

1. *Public authority.* The resort to force must be a public act on behalf of a political community that has been seriously wronged.

2. *Just cause.* "The damage inflicted by the aggressor on the nation or community of nations must be lasting, grave, and certain" (*CCC* 2309). Just cause traditionally includes defense against attack (which can be pre-emptive), recovering damages, and punishing evildoers.

3. *Right intention* (which appears again under *ius ad bello*) (see *CCC* 2310). We should also note that "punishing evildoers" is not revenge (vindictiveness), but rather *retributive justice* (even though many people will cause that justice to be accompanied by a spirit of revenge, and this we must tolerate to some extent even as we work against it).

Once these criteria are met, it is theoretically just to wage the war. Three prudential considerations must, however, also be taken into account. Remember that prudence does not come up with an easy answer in advance, but strikes the mean between excess and defect. These criteria remind us why our country cannot enter into every situation in which warfare would in principle be just.

1. *Proportionality* (which appears again under *ius ad bello*). Will the action end more evil than it causes? Will peace be the outcome? Or will it be a "Pyrrhic victory"? (Pyrrhus, king of Epirus, in 279 B.C. won a victory over the Romans but sustained disproportionately heavy losses.)

2. *Reasonable hope of success* (see *CCC* 2309, third point). Here we must first define what "success" means. It is not necessarily total victory. It might mean slowing down the advancing enemy enough so as to allow the civilians to escape the besieged city. In the war against terrorism, it may mean rooting out just enough terrorists to let others know what we're about.

3. *Last resort* (see *CCC* 2309, second point). Is war the last resort, reasonably understood, or are there still other reasonable alternatives?

The terrorists who have recently attacked Americans, for example, are under the mad illusion that their acts are a last resort against the powerful U.S. Their desperation comes from the unfounded conviction that they have a just cause: creeping U.S. hegemony in the Middle East, in the form of (a) our support for Israel at the expense of the Palestinians, (b) our economic interests, and (c) the export of the shabbier parts of the American way of life. There are numerous civil alternatives to deal with whatever aspects of these concerns are legitimate.

These three prudential criteria impress upon us "the evils and injustices that accompany all war" (*CCC* 2307). Even when war is in principle justified, many other options might be preferable, and our "war against terrorism" must (and does) include these: intelligence work, cutting off terrorists' financial capabilities, and the like.

Once all the above criteria are met, and war is declared, the following criteria regarding the actual fighting of the war are to be met (see *CCC* 2312). Again, these are the *Ius in bello* criteria:

1. *Right intent.* *CCC* 2310 notes that "if [the armed forces] carry out their duty honorably, they truly contribute to the common good of the nation and the maintenance of peace." So the motivation should be to establish the common good, not to vent hatred against the enemy.

Here's one important principle to consider, to my mind the most challenging of all the criteria: Never concretely act in such a way that would render future reconciliation impossible. In your own personal battles, think how easy it is to speak to your enemy in such a way that will never be forgotten. Excesses in this regard are tantamount to self-indulgence: allowing oneself the pleasure that comes from "really putting it to" the enemy.

2. *Proportionality.* The actual tactics should bring about more good than evil. Destruction for destruction's sake is to be avoided.

3. *Discrimination.* No *intentional* harm can be done to non-combatants (see *CCC* 2313). Recall the second criteria of the Principle of Double Effect (PDE).

When we think about war, it's important to recall that while maintaining bodily integrity is a good, it is not the highest good. *VS* 53 notes that there are higher goods, such as giving your life for another. Our belief that we are on pilgrimage to our heavenly home will be of immense assistance. While war is a startling phenomenon, it is actually an especially bold version of the human condition, within which death plays an integral role.[4]

While we're on the topic of war and killing, can I tempt you to deal with a very delicate issue, the death penalty? It seems as if the Church is in the process of changing its age-old position on this—everyone is pretty confused!

Two critical items must be grasped at the outset. Be forewarned: Many Catholics will be a bit uncomfortable with one or the other. But also be patient: I am convinced that if we *carefully* work through all the issues, with all the right distinctions, all Catholics, in fact all men and women of good will open to the natural law, will find the present demands made by the Church to be eminently reasonable.

First, the Catholic tradition has maintained an important set of *principles*, principles rooted in the natural law, and these principles have not and will not be abandoned. This first point should assuage the fears of those who think a longstanding tradition is presently being swept away in its entirety. We'll look at those principles in a moment.

Second item: At present, due in no small part to the "culture of death" in which we live, the *application* of these principles on the part of the Church is undergoing dramatic change. Some would argue that the new application, spearheaded by Pope John Paul II's *EV* and incorporated into the *CCC,* need only be "respectfully considered" on the part of the faithful. In truth, however, the new application requires an actual assent, technically called the "religious assent of intellect and will." We studied that a few chapters ago, and we'll review it shortly.

From the outset, we must make a critical distinction regarding the term "longstanding tradition." There has been a profound tradition of *theological reflection* on these issues, and much of that tradition is reflected in what follows below. The *Magisterial tradition* has—and this will amaze many people— not ever pronounced in a definitive way on the issue.[5] So what the current Magisterium is doing is in a sense brand new. It's an exciting time to be a member of the faithful—and all the more reason to attend to these issues with all the right philosophical and theological equipment.

Let's get our equipment up to snuff by reviewing the foundational principles rooted in the natural law, taking the opportunity to forge a number of critical distinctions that are all too easily lost in today's disputatious atmosphere.

First, the State has the duty to exercise *retributive justice.* Most people today confuse retributive justice with vengeance, but there is a critical distinction between the two. Vengeance, or vindictiveness, is that common passion that drives us to "get back" at another person. "He did it to me; wait till I get him."

Retributive justice, on the contrary, means an objective "balancing of the scales" of justice. The thief, for instance, has caused a lack of order in society. He must redress the disorder, and the State has the responsibility to insure that redress, and to insure that it is proportionate to the crime committed. *CCC* 2266 makes clear that the "primary aim" of punishment is precisely this redress.

Quite a challenge! We are simultaneously forbidden to be vengeful and required to exact retributive justice! Sounds like a high ideal.

Pope John Paul II is known for taking the truth in all its splendor and reminding us that we really can live it (see *VS* 103). His "theology of the body" does this in regard to our sexuality, and I think that he's doing the same thing in regard to justice. He wants us to look at our present failures and recognize, as Christ proclaimed, that "it was not like this at the beginning" (see Mt 19:8). And, with God's grace, it really is possible to live our lives in alignment with the truth God gave us in the beginning (see *VS* 22, and also 18).

In our society (and throughout history) we have failed intellectually to distinguish retributive justice and revenge, and often failed morally by letting vindictiveness build up, often exponentially, alongside retributive justice. The media often interview those close to a victim, who understandably seek "closure" but make their tragedy all the worse by venting a steady stream of vindictive sentiments toward the criminal. When whole communities do this together, the act of retributive justice is spoiled, as it were—it is nothing but communal vengeance. This "overlay" of retributive justice with vengeance is one hallmark of the "culture of death," and the Pope's challenge to us is in no small way occasioned by such confusion.

The challenge is to allow love and forgiveness to accompany the act of retributive justice, much as God did with Cain, back "in the beginning." *That's* what it means to "turn the other cheek." It does *not* mean letting people with a debt to pay simply get off free. It means seeking justice, but simultaneously mortifying the spirit of revenge that so easily wells up within us.

Often the New Testament command to "turn the other cheek" is seen as canceling out the Old Testament dictum "an eye for an eye." Rather, "an eye for an eye" meant that retributive justice must be accomplished in just the right proportion: We must find a fair and reasonable way for a wrongdoer to make amends without getting carried away.

Jesus then tells us to take one more step, and a big one it is: In addition to rightly proportioned retributive justice, we are simultaneously to forgive those who have wronged us. "Forgive us our trespasses, as we forgive those who trespass against us." As the prayer of St. Francis puts it, "It is in pardoning that we are pardoned."

There is a kind of formula here: Retributive justice plus forgiveness equals the Christian response to crime. I've got the key distinction down, between retributive justice and revenge. Now, how do we determine "rightly proportioned retributive justice"? Many say it can never involve death, because only God can take a life.

Many think erroneously that the use of the death penalty would violate the commandment not to kill. But that commandment tells us not to murder, that is, not intentionally to kill the *innocent*. One proportionate way to balance the scales of justice is for the murderer to yield his very life, as affirmed in Genesis 9:6-7, for that criminal has lost his *innocence*.

Think of it this way: A child has perfect innocence, even when getting into mischief. As we begin to make use of our rational faculties, we become more responsible, and when we do wrong we "chip away" at our innocence—we become guilty. We sense profoundly the need to balance the scales of justice; we *need* to make amends.

Think of times you "got away" with a wrong act. No one noticed that you didn't quite pay all the money back, or that you drove your car recklessly. To regain your innocence, you found a way to expiate your guilt. You donated extra to charity or went out of your way to help someone else.

Now consider the criminal who has intentionally killed an innocent person. Imagine the criminal "comes to his senses" and feels the full weight of guilt. He realizes that to balance the scales of justice, he must expiate in a way truly proportionate to his act. He has lost his innocence in the most grievous of ways.

The criminal has dispossessed himself. He is in a position where it would be *appropriate that he lose his life*. And if he were not to lose his life, there would have to be another proportionate mode of justice, such as life imprisonment.

The very existence of the death penalty as a legitimate option—even if never used—is a recognition of the basic moral distinction between innocence and guilt. It is actually a sign of the absolute inviolable dignity of human life! Life imprisonment would be another such sign.

Here's a quick quiz: If neither of these two methods of retributive justice were ever used, what message about the value of human life would be sent to society? Answer: Life is cheap. That's why a good part of the Catholic theological tradition upheld the legitimacy of the death penalty, and why the Magisterium, while never officially pronouncing on the matter, allowed it.

Many would be quick to object that no one can lose dignity. Even the most cold-blooded murderer is still created in the image and likeness of God. Of course they are right, but we must distinguish between innocence and dignity.

Innocence can be lost (partially or completely); dignity can never be lost. A person has dignity by virtue of being a person; though he can act contrary to his dignity, he cannot lose his dignity. That is why every effort should be made to treat prisoners as persons, not objects.

The Church's perspective is changing the way I look at criminals! It never had occurred to me that I was required to forgive them. I now see that forgiveness is essential, *alongside* justice. If we could communicate this to criminals, wouldn't it have a profound effect on them?

Just as we need both to exercise retributive justice and to offer forgiveness, the prisoner needs to *be receptive* to both. Prisoners can live in accord with their dignity by accepting their penalty and facing their penalty with fortitude. They are then *acknowledging* their loss—partial or complete—of innocence.

As *CCC* 2266 notes, when the punishment "is willingly accepted by the guilty party, it assumes the value of expiation.... [It] has a medicinal purpose: as far as possible, it must contribute to the correction of the guilty party." At that point, the prisoner is in a position where he can seek forgiveness—and that forgiveness ought to be ready and waiting for him.

That's where society plays a key role in the rehabilitative process. Rehabilitation is, after retribution, the second purpose of punishment.

Can the rehabilitative purpose of punishment be met if the death penalty is used? A sinner may very well amend his life knowing that the death penalty awaits him. Conversion is the highest mode of rehabilitation.

But society takes a big risk here. While imminent death may well, as someone has said, "concentrate the mind," it can also harden a person. This is the case all the more so if the death penalty is used as retributive justice *without* the accompanying forgiveness—a highly likely scenario in our culture of death.

As Christians we must *will* the conversion of the sinner and offer forgiveness. That's easy when the sin is slight, but the real challenge comes when the sin is grave. *CCC* 2267 states that death takes away the possibility of the criminal "redeeming himself." This statement would seem to suggest not only conversion of heart (which can happen on death row) but an actual "new life"—spent behind bars—in which some genuine contribution is made by a repentant person to society, certainly the society within the prison.

I never realized how much was involved in the exercise of justice! The State sure has an awesome responsibility. I wonder—is our own civil government capable of all this?

Yes, the State plays a rather "kingly" role in all this. It exacts retributive justice, paves the way for rehabilitation, and should also, primarily through the support of religious institutions, encourage the citizenry to mortify the spirit of revenge. As we gaze on the State's awesome task, it becomes a bit clearer what it means to say that the State is a sharer in God's authority (Rom 13:4-5; 1 Pt 2:14), and thus is an instrument of God in exercising justice.

Should the death penalty be necessary in rare cases, it is not as though the State possesses the right to kill. Rather, that task is given to the State, just as the State's authority to legislate is given. The State legislates not by its own power, nor by a power given to it by the will of the majority, but by the natural law whose author is God.

It is arguable that a State which has completely foresworn this understanding of its authority then yields its privilege of acting as the instrument of God. Liberal societies have, it can be argued, abandoned this traditional understanding of the State, insofar as they have abandoned the natural law—consider our abortion laws, for example. Isn't it hypocritical for the State, with one hand, to ignore its own source in natural law, allowing the killing of untold numbers, and with the other hand to execute retributive justice using death—an act that can only be justified under the auspices of the natural law?[6]

If the State has the right from God to use the death penalty, it certainly does not have the duty. When to use and not to use is a prudential decision. We can appreciate each point of the natural law reviewed thus far, points which would support the State's judicious use of the death penalty, and simultaneously assent to the pope's teaching that it would be unwise to use it.

For instance, in a culture where racism is paramount, it would be unwise to use the death penalty because the chances of impartiality are so low. Pope John Paul II, without repudiating the traditional Catholic position, argues similarly that in a "culture of death" we must find other means, bloodless means, of retributive justice. *CCC* 2267 says that such means are more in keeping with the "concrete conditions" of the common good—not the common good in an ideal sense, in which there is total fairness and no vindictiveness, but the common good as it actually plays out within sinful humanity.

Alongside the duty to exact retributive justice and aid in the rehabilitation of the criminal, the State has the duty to defend society. *CCC* 2263–65 emphasizes the importance of legitimate self-defense as "a grave duty for one who is responsible for the lives of others. The defense of the common good requires that an unjust aggressor be rendered unable to cause harm."

The third purpose of punishment, then, is protection of society. Deterrence, the fourth and final purpose, is closely aligned with protection, for the best protection is preventative protection. (By the way, it is in these final two purposes that the Church's teaching on just punishment and her teaching on just war coincide.)

You said at the outset that we needed to be prepared with the right philosophical and theological equipment. I think I'm ready! Exactly what does the Church presently teach about the use of the death penalty? There seem to be two extreme reactions: Some say all Catholics must be in favor of abolishing the death penalty, and others say we can hold what we want as long as we have considered the pope's "opinion."

On this matter we're blessed to have the insights of someone who is both a Cardinal and a top-rate theologian: Avery Cardinal Dulles.[7] He interprets *EV* and the *CCC* to mean this: If society *can* meet the four purposes of punishment—retributive, rehabilitative, protective, and deterrent—with bloodless means such as life imprisonment, then society *ought* to do so.

The reason we ought to take this stance is not because the death penalty is intrinsically evil. It certainly isn't. Rather, it is more prudent to take such a stance given the current culture of death.

EV and the *CCC*, however, seem to let *one* of the purposes of punishment assert itself above the rest—the protection of society. Why not allow all four purposes to be considered? Perhaps because the other purposes can be met just as well, if not better, by life in prison without parole. It is arguably a tougher form of retributive justice, a great source of deterrence, and an option allowing rehabilitation broadly considered.

We owe, I believe, a "religious assent of mind and will" to the Magisterium's teaching. Remind yourself of the different levels of assent we studied in chapter five. We owe an "assent of faith" to infallible teachings like the Trinity and the nature of the sacraments.

On the death penalty issue, certain fundamental principles are taught infallibly, such as the nature of justice and the dignity of the human person. But whenever the Magisterium applies truths about God and humanity to the temporal order (the political, economic, and cultural spheres), those applications do not by definition require an assent of faith. After all, history changes, and the Church must re-apply her teachings accordingly.

That is just what Catholic social teaching does. It applies truths about the human person, the nature of society, culture, and the State, to the ever-changing vicissitudes of history. These applications often require the religious assent of mind and will.

Now for a critical point. Recall that the teaching in the *CCC*, which is a prudential application of certain truths to our current historical context, tells us we must use non-lethal means when the purposes of punishment can be thus met. Note that there is an additional level of prudential judgment needed in *concretely* applying that prudential stance in specific situations: It remains a prudential judgment as to whether or not the protective purpose of punishment can be met, in a specific case, with bloodless means.

The fact that there are "two levels" of prudential application here is critical. On the first level, the Magisterium asks us to assent to its stance. On the second, highly concrete level, each case must be judged separately.

Gaudium et Spes 43 noted that in just such matters—the actual application of a teaching to concrete cases—disagreement among the faithful is to be expected, and the clergy are not to be approached as if they had the right judgment for each case. The clergy safeguard and promulgate the Church's "expertise in humanity" (*SRS* 41), which the laity, as experts in the various spheres of the temporal order, must conscientiously apply.

GS 43 goes on to note that when such expected disagreement occurs, the laity must remember two things: (1) Don't treat one particular application as the only "Catholic" view. (2) Be charitable.

NINE

"THERE IS NO UPPER LIMIT": THE VIRTUES

I keep thinking about that text in *VS* that speaks of the "lower limit" of the moral life, and that is where we would locate the material of the past two chapters—on moral objects and on conflict cases. *VS* makes clear that the inexhaustible, endless "upper reaches" of the moral life are even more important. Can we devote some space to that?

Best for last! And that is what Pope John Paul is getting across in his use of the parable of the rich young man, who is willing to follow all the commandments but hesitates in the face of the demanding and inexhaustible life of moral virtue. We have touched on the virtues throughout the book, and it is only fitting to treat them more systematically as we near the end of our inquiry.[1]

Since we can understand the virtues from the viewpoint of human nature—the natural moral virtues—as well as from the angle of divine grace—the "infused-by-grace-virtues"—this topic will serve us well in recapitulating a central theme of our inquiry: Grace envelops nature, but does not extinguish nature. Catholic moral theology does it all. It maintains the centrality of grace without sacrificing the valuable and useful philosophical dimension of the moral life that focuses on human nature.

Let's begin by discussing the "cardinal" moral virtues of *pru-*

dence, justice, temperance, and *fortitude.* They are called "cardinal" from the Latin word for "hinge," (*cardo, cardinis*) since the whole life of natural virtue "pivots" on these four key virtues. Think of these as "grooves" in your life that keep you headed toward your final destiny. Every particular virtue—patience, magnanimity, gratitude, trustworthiness—belongs to one of these grooves.

In our study of conscience, we distinguished the true or false conscience on the side of the intellect (the "navigator") from the good or bad conscience on the side of the will (the "pilot"). It is in the development of the *true* conscience that *prudence* plays its role. What does it mean in this or that particular case to act justly, or charitably? We know for sure that we must avoid the intrinsically evil acts that are part of the moral "bedrock," but beyond that, prudence helps us discover "just the right way" to act. Let's take the second cardinal virtue, justice, as an example.

Justice is the habit by which the will easily chooses to treat others well. Prudence "attaches" itself to justice so as to practice it in just the right way. For instance, friendliness to others is part of justice. But the person who smiles all the time is excessively friendly, which can turn out to harm relations with others who never know when that individual is in fact unhappy and in need of some type of help.

On the other hand, the person who barely forces out a weak smile or kind word is defective in friendliness. The right balance must be struck, and prudence is the ability to know that middle point. This middle point is called the "mean" of virtue, lying between excess and defect.

To strike the perfect mean between excess and defect does

not mean, however, that we can be *moderately* virtuous. We cannot be chaste some of the time, or courageous some of the time. Rather, we must be chaste and courageous all the time, a task which requires hitting the "mean."

For good examples of particular virtues that fall under the cardinal virtue of justice, turn to the "Scout Law" of the Boy Scouts. There you'll find virtues such as trustworthiness, respect, honesty, loyalty, friendliness, obedience, and courtesy.

Can we try out the "middle point" on the virtue of temperance? I believe that's another of the cardinal virtues.

Yes—the moral virtue of *temperance* (or moderation) perfects our appetites toward things pleasurable. The technical term for that appetite is the *concupiscible appetite*, not to be confused with concupiscence, though they are related. By the wound of *concupiscence* we find it difficult to control our concupiscible *appetite*, as well as other appetites.

While concupiscence is a tendency toward evil (disorder), the *concupiscible appetite* itself is not evil. Pleasurable things are great—so long as they are properly ordered. Temperance allows us to use the pleasurable goods of the world in a proper and ordered way.

Someone who utterly disdains material goods practices temperance on the side of defect, since the creation is good and meant to be used and enjoyed. Someone who takes various goods of creation and misuses them, or makes them into the final end, is on the side of excess. Prudence assists temperance in helping find the proper mean between excess and defect.

Temperance is too often given a very narrow, heteronomous meaning—curtailment, curbing, repressing. But if we look at it through the lens of participated theonomy, it is a key to unlocking authentic freedom. It is a directing of reason in the widest sense: getting all the goods of human life properly ordered under the highest good.

Without temperance, created goods easily "creep up" and vie for the position of the ultimate good. When a created good takes that position, something disastrous happens: The desire for that created good becomes *insatiable*. A person is, after all, treating it as the ultimate good, and that is a position no created good can ever fill. But the person will be endlessly absorbed in the effort. He or she will remain restless until the true ultimate good is placed back where it belongs.

As I'm sure you've noticed, there is something interesting that God built into life to remind us of all this. When we experience created goods, even at their very best, they leave us unfulfilled. Remember the childhood experience of discovering that all the perfect Christmas gifts still leave us wanting something more? That painful experience, and all the adult versions of it, turns out to be friendly to us, reminding us gently (or not so gently) of the *true* ultimate end.

Ouch! It takes a lot of guts to recognize that fact, no?

And you've just hit upon the fourth and final cardinal virtue, *fortitude*. Fortitude (or bravery) is needed to carry out every virtuous act—as you said, it takes "guts" to keep all the goods of life in proper order. We all experience, in different ways, the inertia that lets us "dodge" that proper order.

There's a perfect name for the appetite that says, "Run away from this!" It's called the *irascible* appetite. And there's a virtue—fortitude—by which we can perfect this appetite.

For instance, if you see the importance of studying Latin, but feel overwhelmed by its difficulty for you, you are affected by the irascible appetite (the appetite that says, "Run away from this!"). Fortitude is the virtue allowing you to overcome this barrier and bravely set out to do what is difficult. It also allows you to pursue what is good but dangerous.

Prudence assists fortitude in knowing the proper mean. For instance, jumping in the water to save a drowning swimmer requires fortitude. If I jump in but can't swim myself, I have erred in the direction of excess. People might say I was brave, but in fact I was rash. Or, if I am afraid to jump in, and then do nothing else to help, I err by defect, and I am rightly called a coward.

If we take a bird's-eye view of the four cardinal virtues, we see that ultimately they all work together, getting us in that "groove" toward our final end. We distinguish the different virtues only to unite them in the end. All the virtues need prudence to find the mean; in carrying out any virtue, fortitude and temperance are needed; and they all help us to treat others the right way—which is justice. When we grow in virtue, all the cardinal virtues grow together, just as each finger on a hand grows as the hand grows.[2]

Read *CCC:* 1803–11.

I love seeing the virtues so expansively, in light of our final destiny. But don't a lot of people, upon hearing the word "virtue," think primarily of sexual purity?

Even the word *purity* itself has a much more expansive meaning. Purity is the perfect descriptive term for what our hearts and minds look like if everything in our lives is ordered under and toward the ultimate destiny. We can only arrive at our ultimate end, the Beatific Vision, if we are purified of everything that is incompatible with God's grace.

As the *CCC* notes, "purity of heart is the precondition of the vision of God" (2519). St. John of the Cross compares our souls to windows, which unless pure and clean cannot fully receive the light of God's love nor see that light. The pure heart is the undivided heart that wills what is true loyally and unreservedly.

The *Catechism* points to three specific aspects of purity. The pure of heart are those who "have attuned their intellects and wills to the demands of God's holiness, chiefly in three areas: charity; chastity or sexual rectitude; love of truth and orthodoxy of faith" (2518). Note that the first area is the central aspect of participated theonomy—*charity*, or sanctifying grace. The pure person is irradiated with Christ's grace.

That irradiation has a profound effect on our thoughts, and for that reason we can also speak of purity specifically in regard to the mind. Such purity concerns not only unchaste sexual thoughts but thoughts of envy, greed, covetousness, pride, and so on. Such thoughts compete with God for our loyalty, so we need to be vigilant over them lest they gradually possess us, taking priority over God.

An important distinction is in order here so as to avoid scrupulosity: The impure thought that enters the mind may well be neutral, so long as a person does not *intentionally* put himself in a situation that invites the thought. There is no reason to feel guilty about such thoughts.

It is the choice to dwell on the thoughts—to entertain them (and be entertained by them)—that is inordinate and sinful. As the *Catechism* notes: "Emotions and feelings can be taken up into the *virtues* or perverted by the *vices*" (1768; see the whole section on the passions, 1763–1770).

The second aspect of purity mentioned in the *CCC* is *chastity*. Here we turn directly to sexuality. The chaste person is one who has integrated—properly ordered—sexuality into his or her state in life, be it marriage, celibacy/virginity, or the period in which the person is making a choice about his or her state.

Chastity, far from a heteronomous imposition, is essential to authentic freedom. By it, we are in control of our sexual appetite rather than the other way around. This splendid example of participated theonomy is manifest in *CCC* 2350: "Those who are *engaged to marry* are called to live chastity in continence. They should see in this time of testing a discovery of mutual respect, an apprenticeship in fidelity, and the hope of receiving one another from God. They should reserve for marriage the expressions of affection that belong to married love. They will help each other grow in chastity."

It's just like any other apprenticeship. If you don't master the skill, it will be hard going on the job. If chastity is not in full development before marriage, it will be very hard to develop after marriage.

The "apprenticeship" perspective is enormously important

for helping young people discerning their vocation. Too often, young people think that if they have a good dose of libido, they probably aren't called to celibacy. But *everyone* is called to master sexual passion, in preparation for either the married state or the celibate state. Only when sexual passion is under control is a person *fit* to make a mature decision about *either* marriage or celibacy.

Your whole point is that good things must be used just the right way. That means a fair amount of renunciation. But lots of people think that renunciation is for things that are *bad*—a person who fasts, they say, thinks food is bad, or the celibate person thinks sex is bad. Can you help with this conundrum?

Let's focus on celibacy, especially since so many people today think it is unhealthy and the cause of lots of problems in the Church. Contrary to popular opinion, celibacy is not the suppression of sexuality due to the inherent "badness" of sexuality. Celibacy is very different from abstaining from something because that thing is evil (for example, drugs used for entertainment and pleasure). The celibate is not suppressing a bad thing, but abstaining from a good thing, *precisely so as to recognize its true goodness.*

As Pope John Paul II noted: "When human sexuality is not regarded as a great value given by the Creator, the renunciation of it for the sake of the kingdom of heaven loses its meaning" (*FC* 16). The celibate person is a living, bodily sign that the only way to truly appreciate and enjoy the goods of creation is to keep those goods subordinate to the highest good, the kingdom of heaven.

Compare celibacy to the practice of fasting. We do not fast because food is evil. As St. John Chrysostom said: "What appears good only in comparison with evil would not be particularly good."[3] Anyone who thinks food—or any other part of creation for that matter—is evil is insulting God, whose creation is intrinsically good.

We don't fast because food is bad, but rather because food is not the *highest good*, and—here's the clincher—we cannot truly appreciate the goodness of food until we subordunate it to the highest good. That means being in control of our desire for food (rather than having it control us). Otherwise it loses its taste (no pun intended).

Likewise with sex. It only retains its goodness, and yields genuine happiness (for the soul as well as the body), when it is not in control, but is rather controlled. That's why couples who save sex for marriage, far from being repressed, enjoy sex more, as studies have shown.

This basic principle applies as well to all the goods of creation. The autonomous person ruins those goods by making them into gods; the heteronomous person ruins those goods by disdaining them. Only through participated theonomy do the goods of creation find their proper place, ordered under the highest good, where they can truly be enjoyed.

Those things that are pleasing to our senses are good when used properly. But when misused, they can become a miniature "god" for us.

Consider the person who so desperately needs a certain food, a cigarette, alcohol, or drugs, that he says, "I'll do (just about) *anything* to get it." He has made that created good into his ultimate end, something for which he will do anything. He has made it into his god and thus commits idolatry, violating the first commandment. And he is miserable.

To keep our priorities straight, it's a good habit to abstain from various goods—again, not because they are tainted with evil, but to remind us *concretely* that they are not ultimate goods. (The whole season of Lent is such a reminder.) St. John Chrysostom again: "It is something better than what is admitted to be good that is the most excellent good."

We are truly happy with such goods only when they are properly ordered under the highest good. When we make them our ultimate good, we become miserable—slaves to our passions. True happiness and freedom come from placing the good and the true in spot number one.

This is one of the reasons why natural methods of family planning are so important in marriage. Such methods require a (hefty) dose of abstention, which acts as a constant reminder to the couple that sexual pleasure, while a great good meant to be enjoyed in the task of transmitting new life, is not the "be all and end all" of marriage. Men are particularly vulnerable to falling into this trap—and they become miserable when they do, wreaking havoc on the marriage and the family in the process.

Now imagine that a lifestyle existed which by its very nature was a visible sign to humanity that *despite the wonderful goodness of creation, our ultimate purpose lies beyond this world.* A visible indicator about how truly to enjoy the goods of creation by subordinating them under that ultimate good. In fact, celibacy is that lifestyle, that concrete sign to humanity.

The celibate person *in his or her very bodily existence* is a sign to humanity of the "pearl of great price" (see Mt 13:45) that alone makes life worthwhile. That's why everyone desperately needs to appreciate what that gift signifies. Pope John Paul II sums it up: "Virginity or celibacy, by liberating the human heart in a unique way [see 1 Cor 7:32-35], 'so as to make it burn with greater love for God and all humanity,' bears witness that the kingdom of God and his justice is that pearl of great price which is preferred to every other value no matter how great, and hence must be sought as the only definitive value" (*FC* 16).

So the celibate person is not denying or suppressing sexuality, but burning it in a crucible so that it may be transformed into something higher. We live in a good creation, but we are made for that which transcends it. This is why every created good, wonderful as it might be, leaves us unfulfilled.

As St. Augustine said, "Our hearts are restless, O God, till they rest in thee." The celibate's life signifies all this. That's why celibacy is called an *eschatological sign*. "Eschatological" means "in reference to the last things, the heavenly things, the final goal of all creatures." As John Paul II notes:

In virginity or celibacy, the human being is awaiting, also in a bodily way, the eschatological marriage of Christ with the Church, giving himself or herself completely to the Church in the hope that Christ may give himself to the Church in the full truth of eternal life. The celibate person thus anticipates in his or her flesh the new world of the future resurrection (Mt 22:30).

Without this sense of the eschaton, our lives are miserable because we try to find happiness where it cannot be found. We can be happy in this world and in the next life only by ordering every facet of our existence under our ultimate end.

Goods not so ordered quickly become insipid. Once again: When we demote the highest good, and then try to "stuff" the gaping emptiness with something that cannot possibly fit the bill, we find that our desire for that created good (such as pleasure, wealth, prestige) is insatiable, which ultimately makes it disgusting to us.

Even marriage, as great a good as it is, cannot make us absolutely happy. Anyone who thinks it can places an undue burden on his or her spouse. As a sacrament it is very good, but it is not our ultimate fulfillment. It is only a means toward that fulfillment.

Marriage remains *grounded* in creation in that its purpose has to do with creatures (children), and the intimate partnership of the couple signifies God's love for creation. So one of the most healthy attitudes in a good marriage is the realization that it cannot make you completely happy. What an irony!

Learning about the whole tradition of virtue is illuminating, but scary. Is there any way at least a few of these virtues could be directly infused into us without all the practice?

To give a professorial answer, yes and no. The bad news is that you have to practice: Grace does not cancel nature, but presupposes it. A person's vices don't nicely fall away like scales when that person receives the grace of Christ.

The good news, however, is that all the natural virtues a person has can be infused with Christ's grace, raising them to a supremely high level. These infused-by-grace moral virtues then do wonders for helping a person cooperate with grace to conquer remaining vices.

When people perform virtuous acts, they might have any number of ends in mind. They may be fulfilling themselves, since virtuous people are happy people. Or they may be contributing to the common good, since people are happier when they are around virtuous as opposed to less-than-virtuous individuals. (Think of the exhausted clerk who still gives a smile.)

Nevertheless, the *ultimate* end of a virtuous act is our final end, union with God for eternity. If we are ordered toward that end, it is due to the gift of God's grace inhering in us, called charity. When the natural moral virtues are directed toward the ultimate end, they are then infused with that very charity, and without losing their natural dimension they are lifted up to a higher, transcendent or supernatural dimension.[4]

Only when the moral virtues are infused this way do they come into the fullness of real virtue. Without charity, they are only virtues in a qualified sense. That is why charity is called the "queen" of the virtues, and also the *form* of the virtues.

It's now easy to see why a person who becomes a Christian doesn't instantaneously become a virtuous person. He or she has the indwelling of charity. But until the arduous work occurs of cooperation with grace to develop natural virtues, charity has nothing on which to work. (It certainly can't work on the privation of virtue, or what we call *vice*).

If the "infused-by-grace moral virtues" allow a person to be directed toward the final end, what is the effect on other people? Does that effect remain identical to the effect of the natural virtues?

Now that, with the virtue of charity, I am ordered toward my final end, I can love other people with the love of God that has been poured into my heart. Loving other people with this love means caring for them with their final end in view—as God cares for them. With this love, I will always want my neighbors to follow the moral law no matter how difficult, and I will not assist them in breaking it.

In this light, the great biblical saying "Love your neighbor as yourself" takes on its true meaning. If I genuinely love myself, I am concerned ultimately with my final end, and I orient my whole life toward it. I can only thus love myself if I have the gift of charity. To love my neighbors as myself means to be likewise concerned for them—not just with their temporal comfort and well-being, but with their eternal destiny.

Alongside charity, there are two other infused theological virtues: *faith* and *hope*. Faith is the intellectual assent to the truths revealed by God, while hope is the confidence that we will be able to reach our final goal. Like the moral virtues, these virtues are not full virtues unless infused with charity.

When faith is infused this way, we then possess by participation the very thing believed in: the Trinitarian life. In the same way, when hope is infused with charity, what is hoped for is already present *proleptically* (by anticipation).

Read *CCC:* 1812–32.

Since we're almost to the end, give me one last try at stumping you. If I lose charity—the queen of the virtues—due to mortal sin, then faith and hope are obviously lost as well. Isn't it true, then, that I would have no motivation to get back on track again because I would no longer even believe in any of this, much less hope for it?

Good try. You might have stumped me had I not just read St. Thomas on this very point (I-II, q. 65, a. 4). Recall by analogy how the moral virtues remain, as virtues-in-a-qualified-sense, when a person has lost charity.

The patient person still exhibits patience—good habits, like bad habits, die hard—but those patient acts are no longer ordered toward the final end. Likewise with faith and hope: Without charity, they still can exist, but what is believed in and hoped for is no longer present in the soul. Sanctifying grace is absent.

We call them "dead" faith and hope, or "unformed"(by charity) faith and hope. They still do someone enormous good: Because the person still believes and hopes, he or she is motivated to get back on track, with charity, on the path to his or her final beatific end.

CONCLUSION
"WHERE DO I GO FROM HERE?":
TO THE EUCHARIST

Throughout our inquiry into the good life we have considered the relationship between a "natural" morality that all people can practice, based in a philosophical understanding of nature and the natural law, and a theologically based morality that takes Christian revelation into full account. In the last analysis, though, there are not two types of ethics, one natural and one Christian, any more than there are two types of moral virtues, those natural and those infused with grace. People are either on the trajectory to their final end, or they're off pursuing some out-of-order good as their ultimate end.

If they're on track, they're working on the good life, the virtuous life, and, ready or not, it is infused with grace. Grace encompasses nature. At the same time, they can "pull out" of that one reality a natural component, available philosophically—the natural law and the natural virtues.

As St. Thomas says of the natural virtues, they are really virtues only in a qualified sense. The natural "slice" of the one truth is an important component—grace does not extinguish nature. So if someone were to ask what makes Christian ethics distinctive, the answer would be "wrong question."

Morality is one, with grace infused throughout, in a way that does not extinguish nature. That understood, the only remaining question is to what extent other understandings of morality—secularist, utilitarian, pagan, Buddhist—partake in

Christ's grace. Notice how nothing good and true is excluded from Christian morality, and whatever *is* excluded is "no thing" insofar as it is a privation of what ought to be there but isn't—a lack of due order.

Now it's my turn to come up with a profound insight! Isn't it true that if the only real ethics is a Christian ethics, and if the heart of Christianity is found in the continued sacramental presence of Christ in the Eucharist, then the entire ethical life is related to the Eucharist?

I can't improve on that! But I can lend a few additional distinctions to so profound and startling a truth. Recall the "twin moments" of participated theonomy: We partake in God's order; he pours himself into us. This isn't just a great idea (ortho*doxy*)—it *happens* (ortho*praxis*), and it happens eucharistically.

The moral life both *converges upon* and *flows from* the Eucharist. All moral activity is gathered together and offered to God in the Eucharist, and the grace of the Eucharist makes possible all moral activity. (Read *CCC* 2031—a tremendous text.)

First, the moral life converges upon the Eucharist. Part of what is offered to God in the Eucharist is ourselves, attached to Christ's sacrifice at the offertory of the Mass. We don't offer to God our sinfulness; for that, we ask forgiveness. Our sinfulness cannot be attached to Christ, but is forgiven through and by Christ.

Rather, we offer our healed and elevated natures, along

with the moral activity or moral goodness emanating from them. That moral goodness includes the sometimes staggering sacrifices we are asked to make for the sake of the good, for the sake of Christ. It also includes all the "raw deals" we get in life, raw deals that Christ sanctifies.

The gaping loneliness at the loss of a loved one, the sheer frustration of being saddled with an omnipresent psychological disorder, the limitations imposed by a physical illness or disfigurement—these and the myriad lesser burdens are all presented when we offer our self as a gift. It is right in the context of these "raw deals" that we become "new beings" in Christ, and it is this aspect of ourselves that we offer.

For that reason, Pope John Paul in his encyclical *Redemptor Hominis* speaks of the Eucharist as "the Sacrament in which our new being is most completely expressed" (20). An enormous dignity and integrity flows as we accept the invitation to make ourselves a sacrifice, a sacrifice of praise and thanks.[1] We *participate* in the ultimate expression of God's order.

When you say "Amen" before receiving the Eucharist, you embrace the entire sacramental order of reality safeguarded by the Catholic Church. That pretty well explains why only Catholics in a state of grace should receive the Eucharist.

The second of participated theonomy's "twin moments" is God pouring himself into us. Again, this is not just a great idea (ortho*doxy*) but something you want to *do* (ortho*praxis*). The Eucharist is the source of grace by which we are capable of embracing and living the sacramental life. Christ heals and elevates our natures through his redemptive work (which occurred once and for all on Calvary), and this redemptive grace is made present sacramentally at each moment of history through the Eucharist.

For this reason, the Eucharist is the cause of our new being in Christ. All the "raw deals" of life that we bring and offer at the Eucharist are transformed into the Body of Christ (at the moment of consecration during the canon of the Mass), and it is Christ himself who then nourishes us, pours himself into us, in our reception of the Eucharist.[2]

We then come full circle, having been nourished by the Eucharist, strengthened in our relationship with Christ, further along on the path of holiness, toward our beatific end. We now take this new creation and Eucharistically offer it to the Father, through, with, and in Christ, and in the Holy Spirit, who unifies us with the whole community. With this Eucharistic vision of the moral life, there is no question that the moral law, by which we move on the trajectory toward our final end, is friendly to us, a true participated theonomy.

Introduction: Not Just Academic Reading

1. *Catechism of the Catholic Church*, 2nd ed. (Vatican City: Libreria Editrice Vaticana, 1994, 1997).
2. St. Thomas Aquinas, *Summa Theologica*, trans. Fathers of the English Dominican Province (New York: Benzinger, 1948), (hereafter referred to as *ST*).
3. www.udallas.edu. (Go to "School of Arts and Sciences," then to "Majors," then to "Theology," then to me, "Mark Lowery"— and you'll see the place to click.)
4. All the texts by Pope John Paul II are available from Pauline Books & Media in Boston (the Daughters of St. Paul). Go to www.pauline.org.
5. This text is the focal point of my book. The original text is in *Acta Apostolicae Sedis* 85 (1993), 1133–1228.
6. For all cited Vatican II documents, see Austin Flannery, O.P., ed., *Vatican Council II. The Conciliar and Post-Conciliar Documents* (Collegeville, Minn.: Liturgical Press, 1984); and Walter M. Abbott, S.J., editor, and Msgr. Joseph Gallagher, translation editor, *The Documents of Vatican II* (New York: America Press, 1966).

One
Authentic Freedom and Conscience

1. So, a *voluntary* act (free will) is not necessarily an *authentically free* act, though all truly free acts are also voluntary. See Romanus Cessario, O.P., *Introduction to Moral Theology* (Washington D.C.:CUA Press, 2001), 104.
2. Cessario, *Introduction*, 198, note 15, which refers to Servais Pinckaers' *The Sources of Christian Ethics*. See also Romanus Cessario, *The Moral Virtues and Theological Ethics* (Notre Dame, Ind.: University of Notre Dame Press, 1991), ch. 2.

3. Cessario, *Introduction*, 219, and note the works referenced in footnote 64.

4. See the analysis by Harry Jaffa, *Homosexuality and the Natural Law* (Claremont Institute, 1990), especially 2–6 where he creates a dialogue between Ted Bundy and a soon-to-be-victim. Bundy explains that he is very grateful to his victims, and sees them as making the sacrifices necessary for his happiness, his freedom to live life the way he wishes. To the victim's objection that *her* life is valuable, Bundy replies that that is just her own perspective, and that her life is only valuable to him insofar as it contributes to his happiness. When the victim replies that rape and murder are wrong, Bundy simply invokes the "social contract" notion of freedom, which doesn't recognize moral absolutes. He admits he is breaking the contract, and that he may be caught and punished, but is perfectly willing to take that risk.

5. That which is *essentially* true is also *existentially* true. See Karl Rahner, "On the Question of a Formal Existential Ethics," *Theological Investigations* 2 (Baltimore, Md.: Helicon, 1963), 217–34. Rahner notes that our uniqueness means that our actions really matter—they last eternally (see 227–28).

6. Radio Message of March 23, 1952.

7. These two notions, human person and human nature, exist in harmony and ought never be bifurcated. For a position that falsely bifurcates the two, see Richard Gula, *Reason Informed by Faith: Foundations of Catholic Morality* (New York: Paulist Press, 1989), (hereafter referred to as *RF*), 63.

8. See St. Thomas, *ST* I-II, q. 6, a. 8, "Does Ignorance Cause Involuntariness?" That is to ask, if a person is ignorant of the evil of a particular act, would that imply that he did not will the evil, that the evil was done involuntarily?

9. Here, consult two articles in *ST*: "Is the will evil when it is at variance with erring reason?," which is to ask whether an erring conscience binds (I-II, q. 19, a. 5) and "Is the will good when it abides by erring reason?," which is to ask whether an erring conscience excuses (I-II, q. 19, a. 6).

10. See Msgr. William Smith, "The Meaning of Conscience," in William E. May, ed., *Principles of Catholic Moral Life* (Chicago: Franciscan Herald Press, 1980), 368.

11. Smith, quoting Jane Fonda.

12. St. Augustine, *Confessions*, book II, especially 4–10.

13. See *St. Thomas, ST* I, q. 79, a. 12, as well as I-II, q. 94, a. 2.

14. As Thomas says: "Again, a human act is evil through lacking conformity with its due measure: and conformity of measure in a thing depends on a rule, from which if that thing departs, it is incommensurate" (I-II, q. 71, a. 6).

15. St. Thomas, *ST* I-II, q. 18, a. 1; also q. 5, aa. 1, 3.

16. See Cessario, *Introduction*, 149–58, perhaps the centerpiece of this book.

17. See J. Budziszewski, *The Revenge of Conscience* (Dallas: Spence, 1999), ch. 8 for some great examples.

18. See St. Thomas, *ST* I-II, q. 75, a. 1, ad. 1. Thomas' meditations on sin are found in questions 71 through 89 of *ST* I-II.

19. St. Thomas' *Treatise on Happiness* (in *ST* I-II, qq. 1-5) establishes the existence of this "highest good" toward which all must be ordered if we are to be happy. Thomas shows that wealth, honor, fame, glory, power, bodily goods, pleasure, or indeed any other created good, ultimately cannot fulfill man.

20. "The proper and direct cause of sin is to be considered on the part of the adherence to a mutable good; in which respect every sinful act proceeds from inordinate desire for some temporal good. Now the fact that anyone desires a temporal good inordinately, is due to the fact that he loves himself inordinately; for to wish anyone some good is to love him. Therefore it is evident that inordinate love of self is the cause of every sin" (*ST* I-II, q. 77, a. 4).

Two
Truth Is Friendly to Us: The Meaning of Participated Theonomy

1. Vatican II, *Dignitatis Humanae* 1.
2. The term "moral realism" focuses on the existence of this objective moral law, and the fact that we can really know it and live it. This term is used throughout Romanus Cessario's *Introduction* and is closely connected to the present book's use of participated theonomy. Also see Martin Rhonheimer, *Natural Law and Practical Reason* (New York: Fordham University Press, 2000), 234–56, who uses "participated autonomy."
3. Often we think of heteronomous types as tyrannical, but autonomous types can be the same—both positions are arbitrary, and arbitrariness and tyrannical use of power often go together.
4. See Servais Pinckaers, "The Recovery of the New Law in Moral Theology," *Irish Theological Quarterly* 64 (1999), 3–15.
5. *Decree on Priestly Formation*, art. 16.
6. The *Instruction On Christian Freedom and Liberation* from the Congregation for the Doctrine of the Faith does a splendid job at mining the meaning of the eschaton for Catholic social thought. See especially articles 53, 58, 60–65, and 98.
7. The phrase has appeared in over a dozen important documents in recent years.
8. C.S. Lewis articulates this very point in one of his famous letters from Screwtape—a master devil writing letters of instruction to an apprentice devil trying to lure a convert away from the "enemy" (Christ). In letter VII of *The Screwtape Letters* (New York: Macmillan, 1961), Screwtape discusses whether the convert should be pushed toward Patriotism or Pacifism during the war, and Screwtape says it doesn't matter, so long as Christianity is valued primarily as a means toward one or the other. Lewis' most famous book *Mere Christianity* which has won many converts to Christianity contains this very point in its title. Christianity is not a means to some other end, such that we would speak about "Christianity and self-esteem" or

"Christianity and a more just social order": rather, it is an end in itself—"Mere Christianity."

9. See "Declaration for Concern: On Devaluing the Laity," *Origins* 7, no. 28 (December 29, 1977).

Three
"How Can It Be Wrong When It Feels So Good?": The Natural Law

1. For Thomas, the element within us that is inclined to the Truth is simply called reason, which separates us from the animals. Thomas notes that law—something usually seen as an imposition from without—comes from within: "Law is a rule and measure of acts, whereby man is induced to act or is restrained from acting.... Now the rule and measure of human acts is the reason, which is the first principle of human acts...." (*ST* I-II, q. 90, a.1).

2. See St. Thomas, *ST* I-II, q. 90–97. *VS* 35–46 is the pertinent section on natural law. John Paul II refers to and footnotes St. Thomas in notes 19, 69, 76, 80, 81, 82, and 93. Look up these references, and then find in St. Thomas those precise places on which *VS* relies. Footnotes 69, 76, and 82 all concern the idea that the natural law is a *participation* in divine wisdom.

3. A phrase I first heard from J. Budziszewski, whose books are highly recommended. Also, alongside this chapter you might consider listening to the taped set of lectures by Joseph Koterski, S.J., on the Natural Law, available from The Teaching Company.

4. See St. Thomas, *ST* I-II, q. 93, a. 2 and q. 91, a. 2.

5. *VS* 43, footnoting I-II, q. 90, a. 4.

6. I-II, q. 90, a. 1.

7. Thinkers such as Orestes Brownson and John Courtney Murray, S.J., demonstrate that the Lockean idea of self-ownership, a source used by the founders, runs contrary to their own founding principles. Hence, the American founders built something Catholic unawares.

8. An interesting challenge: How can God have created man "for his own sake" if man's purpose is to give glory to God? Is not man, then, a means to an end, God's end? The conundrum is solved by participated theonomy. While it is true that God has created man for his (God's) glory, that glory is precisely what fulfills man's deepest yearnings. The end toward which God ordained man is, then, something for man's own sake. See John Paul II's *Letter to Families*, art. 9. Also, compare *VS* 10.1 and 13.2.

9. Peter Kreeft, *Making Choices* (Ann Arbor, Mich.: Servant, 1990), 37.

10. St. Thomas sketches these in *ST* I-II, q. 94, a. 2. Some we have in common with all beings, such as "preserve oneself." Others we share in common with the animals, such as procreation and nurture of children (though we bring a distinctively rational dimension to the task). Others are unique to human beings.

11. See Cessario, *Introduction*, 95.

12. This four-step organization is my own method of arranging Thomas' method in I-II, q. 94. See *VS* 51.2. Cessario, *Introduction*, 87–94 has a compatible pedagogy.

13. This intuitive awareness is a genuine knowledge, not a blind feeling resulting in a blind decision. We have a "connatural" sensitivity to moral truths.

14. See St. Thomas, *ST* I-II, q. 94, a. 3: "...[T]o the natural law belongs everything to which a man is inclined according to his nature. Now each thing is inclined naturally to an operation that is suitable to it according to its form: thus fire is inclined to give heat. Wherefore, since the rational soul is the proper form of man, there is in every man a natural inclination to act according to reason: and this is to act according to virtue." Also see q. 94, a. 2, and q. 93, a. 6.

15. Cf. Cessario, *Introduction*, 97–99.

16. See St. Thomas, *ST* I-II, q. 93, a. 6, and pertinent sections in q. 94, articles 4, 5, and 6. Also, see the fine book by J. Budziszewski, *The Revenge of Conscience* (Dallas: Spence, 1999), 22–26.

17. St. Thomas notes in I-II q. 95, a. 1 and q. 96, a. 3 that the law can cause a person to perform acts of virtue, but cannot make him virtuous. After repeated acts of virtue, however, a person may well develop the virtue itself, and in this way the law can be an inducement to virtue.

18. Joseph Koterski, S.J., tape series on the natural law, various places.

19. Thanks not only for the analogy, but for numerous great tips, to Janet Smith.

Four
The Natural Language of the Body

1. See *VS* 50. For example: "Indeed, natural inclinations take on moral relevance only insofar as they refer to the human person and his authentic fulfillment, a fulfillment which for that matter can take place always and only in human nature."

2. For those wishing to explore the relational nature of being philosophically, see the work of W. Norris Clarke, S. J. A fine selection is available in *Explorations in Metaphysics* (Notre Dame: University of Notre Dame Press, 1994).

3. Walter Schu, L.C., *The Splendor of Love* (New Hope, Ky.: New Hope Press, 2003), ch. 5, section 1.d.3.

4. John Paul II, *The Theology of the Body* (Boston: Pauline, 1997), 63, Jan. 16, 1980. This book contains all of John Paul II's Wednesday audiences on the theology of the body. Christopher West has provided an excellent commentary, also from Pauline Press (forthcoming). To immerse yourself in the exciting and life-changing theology of the body, also see the work of Fr. Schu (previous note) and the other works of Christopher West, which include *Good News About Sex and Marriage* (Ann Arbor, Mich.: Servant), and the tape series *Naked Without Shame* (giftfoundation.org).

5. John Paul II, 66, Jan. 16, 1980.

6. When John Paul II speaks of the "genealogy of the human person," he is naming this language: "When a new person is born of the conjugal union of the two, he brings with him into the world a particular image and likeness of God himself: the genealogy of the person is inscribed in the very biology of generation. In affirming that the spouses, as parents, cooperate with God the Creator in conceiving and giving birth to a new human being, we are not speaking merely with reference to the laws of biology. Instead, we wish to emphasize that God himself is present in human fatherhood and motherhood quite differently than he is present in all other instances of begetting 'on earth.' Indeed, God alone is the source of that 'image and likeness' which is proper to the human being, as it was received at Creation. Begetting is the continuation of Creation" (*LF* 9; also see *EV* 42).

7. Listen to the great tape by Janet Smith, "Contraception: Why Not?" (One More Soul, 1-800-307-7685).

8. George Sim Johnston, "Preparing for Marriage," *Crisis* (May, 1998), 13.

9. Cormac Burke, "St. Augustine and Conjugal Sexuality," *Communio* 17 (Winter, 1990), 555.

10. See Paul Quay, *The Christian Meaning of Human Sexuality* (San Francisco: Ignatius), ch. 6 on sexual lies, 64–84.

Five

Partaking in the Divine

1. See *DV* 2; *CCC* 51.

2. St. Thomas indicates several additional reasons why the divine law is necessary, above and beyond the natural law. See St. Thomas, *ST* I-II, q. 91, a. 4.

3. This outline, and similar material, appears in "Infallibility in the Context of Three Contemporary Developments," *Faith and Reason* (1997–98), 225–253, with many additional references.

4. In the recent letter *Ad Tuendam Fidem,* Pope John Paul II made it clear—and fixed it more firmly in Canon Law—that Catholic theologians must align themselves with the Magisterium on all matters of faith and morals. Some further important distinctions are found in that letter, such as the distinction between the primary and secondary objects of infallibility.

5. This is an opportune place to note the relationship between infallibility and truth. All things taught or defined infallibly are true, but not vice-versa. A doctrine can be true without it being taught as true at the level of infallible doctrine. Infallibility signifies not whether or not something is true, but rather a particular weight of authority which the Church places behind various truths that she teaches.

6. See Gula, *RF,* 152–62, who in turn depends on Norbert Rigali.

7. *VS* 109–117 treats the Magisterium, with special attention to the role of service theologians are to provide. Rather than going into the detail given here, the encyclical simply notes that "... the Church's Magisterium also teaches the faithful specific particular precepts and requires that they consider them in conscience as morally binding" (110). The pope used another occasion, *Ad Tuendam Fidem,* to descend into greater detail.

8. See Avery Dulles, "The Hierarchy of Truths in the Catechism," *The Thomist* 58 (July, 1994), 369–88.

9. Dulles, 21.

Six
Disordered Goods: The Mystery of Sin

1. St. Thomas notes that "... passion diminishes sin, in so far as it diminishes its voluntariness" (*ST* q. 77, a. 6).

2. St. Thomas, *ST* I-II, q. 88, a. 1 uses the analogy of health and disease to explain how mortal sin is an irreparable condition whereas venial sin is a reparable disorder.

3. The Church has never given an official, much less infallible,

explanation of the underlying reasons behind the mortal/venial distinction. See John Connery, S.J., "Deliver Us From Evil," in May, *Principles*, 232.

4. On the transcendental level, see: Karl Rahner, "Theology of Freedom," *Theological Investigations* 6 (Baltimore, Md.: Helicon Press, 1969), especially 169; Joseph Boyle, "Freedom, the Human Person, and Human Action," in May, *Principles of Catholic Moral Life*, especially 251–52; Jacques Maritain in "The Immanent Dialectic of the First Act of Freedom," in *The Range of Reason*, 70.

5. God is not one being alongside other beings, but the horizon of being and truth within which all other objects exist. When we know other objects, we invariably know the horizon against which they exist—God—whether consciously aware of it or not. If we try to know that horizon as an object, it eludes us— like the horizon on the ocean, as we approach it moves ahead of us, though it continues to "encompass" us and all beings.

6. Hence, the distinction between psychology and spirituality. Psychology is most helpful in analyzing our experience of reality, whether it be conscious or sub-conscious. Spirituality concerns the deepest, ontological level of the self.

7. Gula, while attempting to avoid the radical extreme, falls into it nonetheless (*RF*, 110–11 and 114).

8. Psychologism is closely linked to what Phillip Reif called the "therapeutic mentality" and what Robert Bellah has called "expressivist individualism." See Reif, *The Triumph of the Therapeutic* (New York: Harper and Row, 1966), and Bellah et al., *Habits of the Heart* (New York: Harper and Row, 1965), especially 32–35, 47–48, and 131–38.

9. There are several fine works available that critique the contemporary capitulation to such a psychologism. See in particular Paul Vitz, *Psychology as Religion: The Cult of Self-Worship* (Grand Rapids, Mich.: Eerdman's, 1977); William Kirk Kilpatrick, *Psychological Seduction* (Nashville, Tenn.: Thomas Nelson, 1983)

and *The Emperor's New Clothes: The Naked Truth About the New Psychology* (Westchester, Ill: Crossway Books, 1985).

10. Gula, *RF*, 30 and 65.

11. One can demonstrate the "necessity" of guilt. If a proponent of psychologism were to say "don't feel guilty," note that in the very word "don't" lies the implicit suggestion that one should feel guilt if one doesn't pay heed to the suggestion at hand.

12. See Karl Stern, *The Third Revolution* (New York: Harcourt, Brace and Co., 1954), 202–208, and the fine summary in Donald DeMarco, *The Anesthetic Society* (Front Royal, Va.: Christendum, 1982), 166.

13. C.S. Lewis, *Mere Christianity*, (San Francisco: Harper, 2001) from the chapter "Morality and Psychoanalysis."

14. A fine book from Ignatius Press—*Battle for Normality* by van den Aardweg—offers a "self-help" method, and an organization called NARTH (*National Association for Research and Therapy of Homosexuality*, www.narth.com) is committed to helping individuals find competent professional help.

15. See Fr. John Harvey, *The Truth About Homosexuality: The Cry of the Faithful* (San Francisco: Ignatius, 1996), ch. 4, for an excellent overview of the many practitioners. Also see the important document from the Catholic Medical Association, *Homosexuality and Hope*, available at www.cathmed.org.

Seven

The Nature of the Moral Act—Making Christ Present in History

1. Better-known proponents include Richard McCormick, Louis Janssens, Josef Fuchs, Bruno Schüller, and Peter Knauer; writers such as Charles Curran, Timothy O'Connell, and Richard Gula have made proportionalist thought accessible to a wide audience. Well-known contemporary defenders (from different perspectives) of the Magisterium's position include William

E. May, Janet Smith, Germaine Grisez, John Finnis, Ralph McInerny, Chris Kaczor and the late Paul Ramsey, and John Connery.

2. Now, one of the hardest texts of St. Thomas is easy to grasp: "Now, in a voluntary action, there is a twofold action, viz. the interior action of the will, and the external action: and each of these actions has its object. The end is properly the object of the interior act of the will: while the object of the external action, is that on which the action is brought to bear. Therefore just as the external action takes its species from the object on which it bears; so the interior act of the will takes its species from the end, as from its own proper object" (I-II, q. 18, a. 6) (*Treatise on Happiness,* trans. John Oesterle; Notre Dame, Ind.: University of Notre Dame Press, 1964). From here, with bolstered confidence the interested reader now hooked on St. Thomas can pursue all of questions 18 and 20.

3. See *ST* I-II, q. 20, a. 4, which shows how the external act can add good or evil to the internal act.

4. A debate has ensued between the Thomistic natural law theory presented here and a "new" natural law theory (not revisionist!) that places more emphasis on the agent's will in assessing human acts. See the web site for more.

Eight
The Tough Cases

1. See the argument presented by Janet E. Smith in "The 'Many Faces of AIDS' and the Toleration of the Lesser Evil," *International Review of Natural Family Planning* (Spring, 1988), 1–15.

2. See May's article on PDE in the *Encyclopedia of Bioethics,* 316–20.

3. See Nathan Schleuter, "Drawing Pro-Life Lines," *First Things* (October 2001), 32–34 (firstthings.com).

4. See C.S. Lewis, "Learning in War-Time," in the collection *The Weight of Glory* (New York: MacMillan, 1980). While you're there, don't miss another great essay, "Why I am not a Pacifist."

5. Prof. Robert Fastiggi explains this distinction in the *First Things* (see note 7 discussion below).

6. This argument is set forth by Steven Long, *"Evangelium Vitae, St. Thomas Aquinas, and the Death Penalty,"* *"The Thomist"*63 (1999), 511–52.

7. *First Things* (April 2001, 30–35) (firstthings.com), and see the correspondence in the June issue. Then see May 2002 for Antonin Scalia, "God's Justice and Ours" (17–21). Dulles and others (e.g., Long, Fastiggi) reply to Scalia, with Scalia's rejoinder, in the October 2002 issue.

Nine
"There Is No Upper Limit": The Virtues

1. St. Thomas' material on the virtues is vast; the serious student will be interested in working through at least certain sections of the questions on virtue in general, found in *ST* I-II, 49–70. The following questions are suggested: 55–58, 61–67. Then, read some of the questions on the theological virtues, found in II-II, 1–46, such as 1–7, 17–21, and 23, 24, and 27. Much of the material in *ST* II-II is devoted to the vast panoply of virtues.

2. *ST* I-II, q. 66, a. 2.

3. *Virginity*, X: PG 48:540, cited in John Paul II, *FC* 16.

4. In my own view, the gifts and fruits of the Holy Spirit (see *CCC* 1830–32) are none other than the infused moral virtues. For another view, see Cessario, *Introduction*, 205–12.

Conclusion
"Where Do I Go From Here?": To the Eucharist

1. Cf. William Cardinal Baum, "The Distinctiveness of Catholic Moral Teaching," in May, *Principles*, 12.

2. Baum, 16.